A GUIDE TO DECISION-MAKING

BY PAUL AJAL

Scripture quotations marked KJV are taken from King James Version of the Bible. Scripture quotations marked NKJV are taken from New King James Version of the Bible.
Copyright © 1979, 1980, 1982 by Thomas Nelson, Inc.

A Guide To Decision-Making
Copyright © 2016 by PAUL AJAL

Tel: +256 787 034 528/+256758824550
Email: Paul.ajal25@gmail.com

ISBN-13: 978-1532753510
ISBN-10: 1532753519

All rights reserved. No part of this book may be reproduced or transmitted in any form or by any means, electronic or mechanical, including photocopying, recording, or by any information storage and retrieval system, without permission in writing from the publishers or the author.

TABLE OF CONTENTS

ACKNOWLEDGEMENTS
INTRODUCTION

CHAPTER ONE
    What is decision-making?   9
CHAPTER TWO
    Factors that influence decision making   15
CHAPTER THREE
    How to test the validity of a decision   25
CHAPTER FOUR
    When do we make a decision?   33
CHAPTER FIVE
    How to deal with Ordeals   35
CHAPTER SIX
    The best way to enter into marriage   46
CHAPTER SEVEN
    Do you want to be an overcomer?   52
CHAPTER EIGHT
    How to register success   56
CHAPTER NINE
    Decision for a Comeback   63
CHAPTER TEN
    Choosing on where to spend Eternity   70
CHAPTER ELEVEN
    Deciding on how to acquire wealth   75
CHAPTER TWELVE
Choosing on whom or what to serve   79

CONCLUSION   95
GLOSSARY   96

ACKNOWLEDGEMENTS

First and foremost, I would like to hold the heavenly Father in high esteem for yet another opportunity He has given me to reach millions of souls through this book. I thank Him also for the grace that enabled me to endure and overcome all the challenges I encountered during the time of writing this book and financial provision which facilitated its publication.

Special thanks also to the following:
Apostle John Mulinde for your life changing messages which inexplicable way have made a tremendous impact on my life.

My Pastors: Peter Oumo, Pius Okiria, Emmanuel Kakaire, Godfrey Bwire, Stephen Nkambwe, Leonard Rwego, Fredrick Isabirye, Joyce Nantongo, Richard Okanya, Fred Kirya of Trumpet Centre Churches; and pastor Osborn Okopa of Obanga pewany Pentecostal Assemblies of God, for your pastoral works which have equipped, fashioned, moulded and produced me to the level of spiritual maturity I am in today.

Mama Mary Mulira together with your children: Paul Mulira, Charles Mulira, Stephen Mulira, Carol Mulira Kasirye, Rita Mulira Muzoora and everyone who is directly or indirectly attached to your family; for gladly accepting me and my wife in your family. I am completely overwhelmed by your kindness, love, care and support. I can't afford also to forget the facilities in your home that I used during the time of writing this book, the peaceful atmosphere that is really very conducive to writing/concentrated study and your words of encouragement that greatly boosted my morale to write this book. May the just God remember all your charitable deeds that you have shown towards me and my wife. May He also beautify you with salvation, open up all the doors of impossibilities, satisfy you with long life so that your entire family may be noted for longevity - even for generations after you; and may He be unto you according to His words and promises.

Edith Mukidi together with your children: Maurice Kiddu, Fiona Kazairwe, Marion Nakazi, Moreen Namutebi and Lorna Kainju; for adopting my wife as a daughter in your family and for infusing the Christian qualities into her life - which qualities have left a positive influence in her life! The blessings, joy, peace and favour which I now enjoy in our marriage are attributable to your great efforts. I would like also to thank you for your unwavering support, sincere love and prayers which besides other results have also given birth to this book. May God who answers prayers meet you at the point of your needs. And may He ascribe to you blessings, prosperity, joy, peace, fortunes, favour and long life.

To my dear wife Maria Ajal, for always is behaving in the Christian way. Dearest, the Christian qualities in you have really played a big role in consolidating our marital relationship. And as people say, "behind a successful man there is a strong woman", it's really the case with me; for the strength of your prayers, your words of encouragement and counsel have always shown me as a successful man. You are an absolute treasure – I promise to love you forever just as we exchanged in our vows, on our wedding day.

INTRODUCTION

Before I knew the truth about decision-making, it had always been uneasy for me to reach a decision and come out with a concrete resolution. For I used not only to struggle with making decisions, but also to make wrong choices and decisions; and sometimes I could fail completely to decide on certain things. And because of this, I made several awful messes in life! But after knowing the truth I have written in this book, my life has never remained the same. Now given many who are increasingly faltering between opinions and are in the valley of decisions, and those who combatively make decisions; I felt it fitting to write a book about decision-making. I am quite sure that this book will "meet a long-felt want of many" and hence, it will also relieve them from flocking counselling sessions.

This is a faithful saying for in this book, I have particularly debated on decision- making; even mentioning how to make right decisions. In this book, you will also find the benefits of making right decisions and the long or momentary effects of making fateful or wrong decisions. I have also in this book catered for those whose lives are in jeopardy as a result of deciding wrongly and even those who are in the point of no return, for I have shown them how they could come out of their messes! I have also given some elements where we have to base our decisions if our decisions should be valid.

For those who are overcome with things like sin, poverty, Satan's power, bad habits and addicts; I have given how they could overcome and become masters over them. For those who intend to enter into marriage, I have given the godly way of handling it. Even those who entered in a wrong way other than godly, I have also given some counsels which could help them mend their ways. Now as you read the chapters of this book, you will discover many things that I could not give all in this introductory part.

But for some words or expressions I have used in this book which you may not be familiar or comfortable with, please advise the glossary on page 96. For in the glossary, I have explained the meaning of some words or expressions just in the context I have used them and they are in alphabetical order.

I beseech you therefore to read the writings of this book carefully, meditatively, prayerfully and frequently. I promise you, in the final analysis you will gain a heart of wisdom that will help you to make right decisions and choices. Even though you were discouraged, your lost hopes shall be revived! It's therefore my earnest prayer that whoever shall read this book should be blessed, equipped, revived and strengthened. And may the Holy Spirit guide whoever shall read this book so that they may grasp the spirit dimension of the writings of this book in Jesus' name. Amen.

CHAPTER ONE
WHAT IS DECISION-MAKING?

Decision-making in my own definition is the ability to decide on something, exercise judgement by showing justice or taking sides; or to solve a problem basing on right or wrong moral, and to come out with a concrete resolution. It takes a decision for someone to do something good or evil, and come out with a tangible result.

The decisions we take could therefore affect us positively or negatively. It could also prosper us temporarily or permanently, or ruin us temporarily or permanently. Many people are what they are today because of their past decisions. In other words, they are the products of their decisions.

We could take decisions jointly as a family, nation, government, tribe, clan, an organization, an ethnic group or individually. Now, whether jointly or individually, but depending on the basis of our decisions; in one way or the other, we shall always be affected. If for instance someone decides to commit suicide, he will for sure die and go to hell. This is an example of a decision based on a wrong moral. There are many decisions we take which are based on wrong morals and their results are always devastating.

Deciding not to forgive, to disobey God, murder, malice, plunder, cheat on your spouse, seek those who are mediums for solutions to your problems, blaspheme God, to mention but a few; are other examples of decisions which are based on wrong morals. Deciding to do good things or taking a decision that is based on right moral is desirable and it always gives a beneficial result. The Bible gives an example of a decision that was taken on right moral by Daniel. This was especially when he decided not to defile himself with the portion of the king's delicacies.

The decision that Daniel took moved God to bring him into the favor and goodwill of the chief of eunuchs. Another result of this decision was that, God gave Daniel wisdom and understanding in all matters. And after king Nebuchadnezzar's interview, Daniel was found ten times better than all the magicians and astrologers who were in all realm of the king!

"But Daniel purposed in his heart that he would not defile himself with the portion of the king's delicacies, nor with the wine which he drank; therefore he requested of the chief of the eunuchs that he might not defile himself. Now God had brought Daniel into the favour and goodwill of the chief of the eunuchs. And the chief of the eunuchs said to Daniel, I fear my lord the king, who has appointed your food and drink, for why should he see your faces looking worse than the young men who are your age? Then you would endanger my head before the king. So Daniel said to the steward whom the chief of the eunuchs had set over Daniel, Hananiah, Michael, and Azariah, "please test your servants for ten days, and let them give us vegetables to eat and water to drink. Then let our appearance be examined before you, and the appearance of the young men who eat the portion of the king's delicacies; and as you see fit, so deal with your servants." So he consented with them in this matter, and tested them ten days. At the end of ten days their features appeared better and fatter in flesh than all the young men who ate the king's delicacies. Thus the steward took away their portion of delicacies and wine that they were to drink, and gave them vegetables."

"As for these young men, God gave them knowledge and skill in all literature and wisdom; and Daniel had understanding in all visions and dreams. Now at the end of ten days, when the king had said that they should be brought in, the chief of the eunuchs brought them in before Nebuchadnezzar. Then the king interviewed them, and among them all none was found like Daniel, Hananiah, Mishael, and Azariah; therefore they served before the king. And in all matters of wisdom and understanding about which the king examined them, he found them ten times better than all the magicians and astrologers who were in all his realm." (Daniel 1: 8 - 20) NKJV

Much as decision-making is of paramount importance, but there are some people who still find it not easy to take decisions. Truly, there are three categories of people who either struggle or fail completely to take decisions. These three categories are: 1) those that are not decisive, 2) those that are not principled and 3) those that waver or falter between opinions.

Those who are not decisive are the ones who do not have the ability to decide quickly even on matters of urgency. They are always surrounded with confusion. Even if they are faced with matters or situations that call for prompt actions, they either rely on other people for decision-making or simply accept defeat and surrender to the will of those things they are faced with. This category of people is carefree even in matters that concern them, and it is really very hard for this category of people to make progress in life.

Those who are not principled are the ones who are not consistent in most of the things they decide on. They cannot also stick to the very decisions they themselves have made. This category of people may decide to do something today, but because of their inconsistency; they may decide again to abandon it just after a short time.

Those who waver or falter between opinions are the ones who hesitate about making a decision or choice. Their hesitancy always put them in the valley of decisions. But being in a valley of decision is a very dangerous thing, and we should always try with our utmost to avoid being in this kind of state.

The Bible gives an account of Prophet Elijah's suggestion to the Israelites of choosing between God and Baal.

> **"And Elijah came to all the people, and said, how long will you falter between two opinions? If the Lord is God follow Him, but if Baal, follow him. But the people answered not a word."**
> **(1 Kings 18: 21) NKJV**

Those who waver or falter between opinions are also the doubtful who do not put faith in the things they do. They are double-minded people who are always unstable in all their ways. The Bible promises nothing to this category of people. For it's written,

> **"If any of you lacks wisdom, let him ask of God, who gives to all liberally and without reproach, and it will be given to him. But let him ask in faith, with no doubting, for he who doubts is like a wave of the sea driven and tossed by the wind. For let not that man suppose that he will receive anything from the Lord; he is a double-minded man unstable in all his ways." (James 1: 5 – 8) NKJV**

Falling in any of the three categories mentioned above is as useless as leading a life with emptiness. If we want to make wise and serious decisions, we should then avoid belonging to any of these categories.

LESSONS TO LEARN FROM DECISION- MAKING

- ❖ Let others advise you, but do not allow them to decide for you.
- ❖ A wise decision comes from a wise counsel.
- ❖ Extraordinary people make extraordinary decisions.
- ❖ Our tomorrow's successes depend on our today's decisions.
- ❖ Unwise people take unwise decisions.
- ❖ Always endeavor to be decisive especially on matters of urgency.
- ❖ Is your life in jeopardy because of the careless decision you took? Take another careful one - it will definitely bail you out!
- ❖ Any uncarefully considered decision will always cost "an arm and a leg".
- ❖ When you fail to decide, then you are deciding to fail.
- ❖ When you are emotionally disturbed, first overcome your emotions before taking any decision.
- ❖ Only those who are in full possession of their mental faculties could reason in a big way, and take meaningful decisions that could produce extraordinary results.
- ❖ Avoid making fateful decisions for their effects will be very bad on your future.
- ❖ When you have decided otherwise, do not take a wrong decision again to solve your problem, just correct the first mistake and remain wise.
- ❖ Are you in the point of no return? Do not hang there - there is still hope for you! Learn from the prodigal son in the Bible and come to your senses. For in your right mind you will make right decisions.
- ❖ Do you want to avoid hell? Decide now to accept Jesus Christ as your Lord and Savior and observe the dos and don'ts of God's word.
- ❖ Do not allow things to get out of hand. If they have gone out of hand, do everything it may take to bring them under control.
- ❖ Decide now to seek the Lord while He may be found. Call upon Him while He is near. For when you tarry, you will seek Him one day and find Him not, you will call upon Him and He will answer not.

- Do you want to avoid regrets, embarrassments, humiliations, disappointments or discouragements? Then learn to base your decisions on right morals.
- Do you want to avoid the impending judgement? Decide now to stop sinning and begin to lead a life of virtue.
- Procrastination is as bad as hardening of the heart, therefore avoid it for it will hinder you from making timely decisions.
- Making a wish is just postponing the problem, but making a decision will give solution to the problem.
- When fate has decided otherwise, just embrace it, do not react otherwise; for fate has got something to do with your destiny!
- When you have decided to do good do not grow weary, nor lose heart; just continue steadfastly for in due season you will reap.
- Do you want God to prove Himself strong on your behalf? It's simple; just decide now to show a loyal heart to Him, for unto such His eyes run to and fro throughout the whole earth!

CHAPTER TWO
FACTORS THAT INFLUENCE DECISION-MAKING

There are many factors that are influential in making decisions, and these factors are a major determinant of the decisions we make. For they can either cause us to make right or wrong decisions. In this chapter of the book, I will give and briefly explain the major ones.

1. THE POWER BEHIND THE THRONE:

The power behind the throne is the person who really controls an organization, a government, country or family in contrast to the person who is legally in charge. According to God's own design, a man is supposed to be the head of the family, and he is expected to play a major role in decision-making. However, given the prevailing emancipation of women, some have gone overboard and taken advantage for evil gains. So then, a family whose power behind the throne is a woman, most of the decisions come from her, and her words are always final. Whether her decisions are good or bad, the man has to go by them for she indirectly rules over him and the entire family.

In the Bible, we are told the story of Jezebel, Ahab's wife; who was the real powers behind the throne in their family and in the reign of Ahab her husband, who was the king of Samaria. Jezebel being very influential did many wicked things both in their family and the reign of her husband. One wicked thing she did during her husband's reign was the plot that claimed Naboth's life simply to take possession of his vineyard!

"And it came to pass after these things that Naboth the Jezreelite had a vineyard, which was in Jezreel, next to the palace of Ahab King of Samaria. So Ahab spoke to Naboth saying, give me your vineyard that I may have it for a vegetable garden, because it is near, next to my house; and for it I will give you a vineyard better than it. Or, if it seems good to you, I will give you its worth in money. But Naboth said to Ahab, the Lord forbid that I should give the inheritance of my fathers to you. So Ahab went into his house sullen and displeased because of the word which Naboth the Jezreelite had spoken to him; for he had said, I will not give the inheritance of my fathers. And he lay down on his bed, and turned away his face, and would eat no food. But Jezebel his wife came to him, and said, why is your spirit so sullen that you eat no food? He said to her, because I spoke to Naboth the Jezreelite, and said to him; give me your vineyard for money; or else if it pleases you, I will give you another vineyard for it. And he answered; I will not give you my vineyard. Then Jezebel his wife said to him, you now exercise authority over Israel! Arise, eat food and let your heart be cheerful; I will give you the vineyard of Naboth the Jezreelite. And she wrote letters in Ahab's name sealed them with his seal, and sent the letters to the elders and the nobles who were dwelling in the city with Naboth. She wrote in the letters, saying, proclaim a fast, and seat Naboth with high honor among people; and seat two men, scoundrels, before him to bear witness against him, saying, you have blasphemed God and the King. Then take him out, and stone him, that he may die. So the men of his city, the elders and nobles who were inhabitants of his city, did as Jezebel had sent to them, as it was written in the letters which she had sent to them. They proclaimed a fast, and seated Naboth with high honors among the people. And two men, scoundrels, came in and sat before him; and the scoundrels witnessed against him, against Naboth, in the presence of people, saying, Naboth has blasphemed God and the King! Then they took him outside the city and stoned him with stones, so that he died. Then they sent to Jezebel, saying, both has been stoned and is dead. And it came to pass, when Jezebel heard that Naboth *had been stoned and was dead, that Jezebel said to Ahab, "A rise, take possession of the vineyard of Naboth the Jezreelite, which he refused to give you for money; for Naboth is not alive, but dead." So it was, when Ahab heard that Naboth was dead, that Ahab got up and went down to take possession of the vineyard of Naboth the Jezreelite." (I Kings 21: 1 -16) NKJV.*

Though Jezebel died long time ago, but her spirit is still in operation. As a matter of fact, there are some men and women in this generation who are possessed with the spirit of Jezebel. They are so influential wherever they are, yet the decisions or advices they give are always wicked!

In government, policy-making body plays a big role in making decision. Through this body, the government may adopt or propose good or bad policies depending on what this body comes out with.

2. FATE:

Fate, which is the power, believed to control events in a way that cannot be resisted, is another factor that is influential in decision-making. Sometimes in exceptional cases, we may decide on something in the way we want, but fate will decide otherwise; so that what we expect – we do not get and what we do not expect is what prevails. When God sent Jonah to Nineveh, he decided to flee to Tarshish away from God's presence. But since it was fate and it could not be resisted, Jonah's course was changed in mysterious circumstance and he found himself in the very place he didn't like to go to!

'Now the word of the Lord came to Jonah the son of Amittai, saying, "Arise, go Nineveh, that great city, and cry out against it; for their wickedness has come up before Me." But Jonah arose to flee to Tarshish from the presence of the Lord. He went down to Joppa, and found a ship going to Tarshish; so he paid the fare, and went down into it, to go with them to Tarshish from the presence of the Lord. But the Lord sent out a great wind on the Sea, and there was a mighty tempest on the Sea, so that the Ship was about to be broken up.

"Then the mariners were afraid; and every man cried out to their god, and threw the cargo that was into the ship in the sea, to lighten the load. But Jonah had gone down into the lowest parts of the Ship, had lain down, and was fast asleep. So the captain came to him, and said to him; 'What do you mean, sleeper? Arise, call on your God; perhaps your God will consider us, so that we may not perish'. And they said to one another, 'come let us cast lots, that we may know for whose cause this trouble has come upon us'. So they cast lots and the lot fell on Jonah. Then they said to him, 'Please tell us! For whose cause is this trouble upon us? What is your occupation? And where do you come from? What is your country? And of what people are you?' So he said to them, 'I am a Hebrew; and I fear the Lord, the God of heaven, who made the Sea and dry land,' then the men were exceedingly afraid, and said to him, why have you done this? 'For the men knew he fled away from the presence of the Lord, because he had told them. Then they said to him, what shall we do to you that the sea may be calm for us?-for the Sea was growing more tempestuous. And he said to them, 'Pick me up and throw me into the Sea; then the Sea will become calm for you. For I know that this great tempest is because of me.' Nevertheless the men rowed hard to return to the land, but they could not, for the Sea continued to grow more tempestuous against them. Therefore they cried out to the Lord and said, 'We pray, O Lord, do not let us perish for this man's life, and do not charge us with innocent blood; for You, O Lord, have done as it pleased You.' So they picked up Jonah and threw him into the Sea, and Sea ceased from its raging. Then the men feared the Lord exceedingly, and offered a sacrifice to the Lord and took vows. Now the Lord had prepared a great fish to swallow Jonah. And Jonah was in the belly of the fish three days and three nights. Then Jonah prayed to the Lord his God from the fish's belly. And he said; I cried out to the Lord because of my affliction, and He answered me. Out the belly of the Sheol I cried, and You heard my voice, for you cast me into the deep, into the heart of the Seas, and the floods surrounded me; all your billows and your waves passed over me, then I said; I have been cast out of your *sight; yet I will look again toward Your holy temple. The waters surrounded me, even to my soul; the deep closed around me; weeds were wrapped around my head. I went down to the moorings of the mountains the earth with its bars closed behind me forever; yet you have brought my life from the pit; O Lord, my God. When my soul fainted within me, I remembered the Lord; and my prayer went up to You, into Your holy temple. Those who regard worthless idols forsake their own mercy. But I will sacrifice to You with the voice of thanksgiving; I will pay what I have vowed. So the lord spoke to the fish, and it vomited Jonah onto the dry land. {Jonah chapters one and two] NKJV.*

3.   RESENTMENT:

Resentment is yet another factor that is influential in decision-making. Resentful people therefore make decisions resentfully. Some people after bearing a deep-seated resentment over the way they were treated in the past, or after experiencing awful moments; they remain tormented with the memories of their past experiences. And because of this torment, any decision they make that is related to what they went through is always negative**!**

4.   STEREOTYPE:

Stereotype is a fixed idea, image or opinion that many people have of a particular type of thing or person, but is often not true in reality. Many people have made negative or wrong decisions, especially on that particular thing or person they are mistaken about, simply because of stereotype. If someone has a stereotype view about another as a bad person, he may then decide to damage the reputation of the one he is mistaken about, or he may develop negative feelings about him. The stereotype view of men over women as housewives has made some men to run into domestic violence. The view that this type of men has, may cause them to take decisions that restrict their wives to only household chores. As for me, this kind of view is unfair and it is completely hypothetical.

5. INFERIORITY COMPLEX:

Inferiority complex also influences the decisions we make. Some people feel too inferior about themselves that they always limit themselves while making decisions. A person who feels inferior about himself or herself is always full of negative beliefs or confessions. This person is ever fond of these kinds of confessions: my life amounts to nothing, I am a walking corpse, I am as good as dead, I am not worthy for anything or I can't make in life. Now when it comes to making decisions, those negative confessions restrain him from making serious decisions.

6. EMOTIONS:

Though emotions are just feelings of bad or good things, they are very influential in decision-making. Emotionally disturbed people therefore take decisions under the influence of emotions. So when we allow emotions like jealously, anger or temperament to overcome us; we may take decisions which we have not considered properly and soon we shall begin to regret.

7. KNOWLEDGE:

One's level of knowledge about somebody or something, will determine the decisions they will make about that particular person or thing. Jesus Christ the Son of God was crucified by the very people He was sent for, because they didn't have full knowledge about Him. The decision they took to do away with the Holy and Anointed One of God was because of ignorance. If really they had known that Jesus Christ was the One they were expecting, then they wouldn't have killed Him. It's therefore advisable to always have full knowledge about that particular person or thing before taking any decision. Where possible we should prayerfully seek God's counsel so that we may get revelations about that particular person or thing. This will obviously help us to take wise decisions.

8. CHARACTER / PERSONALITY:

Character or personality is another factor that is influential in decision-making. One's character or personality will therefore determine the decision he will make. Those who have godly characters, most of the decisions they take are always godly and those who have ungodly characters, most of the decisions they take are ungodly. Ungodly characters do not only cause us to make ungodly decisions, but they also limit us in our decisions.

Those who do not have the character of boldness for instance, lack faith, and most of the decisions that this category of people takes is always surrounded with fear. Those who have dynamic personalities are the ones who can take serious and costly decisions, be it for good or for bad. Being a terrorist or suicide bomber requires a dynamic personality. To bring a change, it requires also those with dynamic personalities.

9. TRADITION:

Traditions, culture, customs or norms are very influential in decision-making. Many people therefore tend to make decisions according to their traditions, culture, customs or norms. When it comes to choice, taste or preference, those who are conservative to tradition will always make decisions in a traditional way. This is so because the traditional attitudes or values they have, are driving forces in the decisions they make.

Apostle Paul in the Bible tells us how he was zealous for the traditions of his fathers.

"For you have heard of my former conduct in Judaism, how I persecuted the Church of God beyond measure and tried to destroy it. And I advanced in Judaism beyond many of my contemporaries in my own nation, being more exceedingly zealous for the traditions of my fathers." (Galatians 1:13-14) NKJV

In the verses given above, Paul's prejudice against the Church of God is clearly seen. What prompted him to persecute the Church of God was his being traditionally bias. Now the traditional attitudes he had could not allow him to tolerate any form of worship or faith other than the one for his fathers!

10. IDEOLOGY:

Ideology is yet another influential factor in decision-making. What one believes in matters a lot when it comes to making decisions. Those who believe in Satan and his power for instance, they rely on him while taking decisions. And those who believe in God and His power, they allow Him to intervene in their affairs and most of the decisions they make - they rely on Him for wisdom and counsel.

11. TRANSFORMATION / DELIVERANCE:

One's level of transformation or deliverance will determine the decisions he will make. When one is not transformed or delivered from some aspects of his life, then those areas will drive him to make wrong decisions. Those who are fully transformed or delivered, they have the mind of Christ. Now instead of deciding to hate those who have wronged them for instance, they decide to forgive and continue to love them!

The Bible urges us to be transformed by the renewing of our minds. **"And do not be conformed to this world, but be transformed by the renewing of your mind, that you may prove what is that good and acceptable and perfect will of God." (Romans 12:2) KJV.**

Transformation is all about renewing one's mind. If our minds are renewed, then the decisions we take shall be different from those whose minds are not renewed. Those whose minds are renewed they have the mind of Christ. Let's therefore allow God to renew our minds so that we may always take right decisions which are pleasing in His sight.

12   WILL:

Will is the most influential factor in decision-making and it's normally what influences any decision we take. Will is in three ways; the will of God, other people's will and the free or permissive will. When we critically look into any decision we take, we shall discover that it just revolve on the three types of will mentioned above. Now God created man and left him with free or permissive will. A man therefore has a great deal of liberty to take any decision he wishes, whether for doing good or evil. Many people ignore God's will while taking decisions and instead rely on other people's will or the free will God has given them. As for me, I would suggest that we use the free will or other people's will to take decisions on simple matters. But on crucial matters, it would be good for us to first seek the mind of God before reaching a decision.

When God created Adam and Eve, He put them in the Garden of Eden and commanded them not to eat the fruit of Knowledge of good and evil. Now Satan being more cunning than any beast of the field, which the Lord God had made, entered through Eve with his subtle strategy. After a little dialogue with Satan, Eve heeded his deceptions and went ahead to eat the forbidden fruit. The decision that Adam and Eve took to eat the forbidden fruit was totally against the will of God.

"Now the serpent was more cunning than any beast of the field which the Lord God had made. And he said to the woman, has God indeed said, you shall not eat of every tree of the garden? And the woman said to the serpent, we may eat the fruit of the trees of the garden, but the tree which is in the midst of the garden, God has said, you shall not eat it, nor shall touch it, lest you die. Then the serpent said to the woman, you shall not surely die. For God knows that in the day you eat of it your eyes will be opened, and you will be like God, knowing good and evil. So when the woman saw that the tree was good for food, that it was pleasant to the eyes, and a tree desirable to make one wise, she took of its fruit and ate. She also gave to her husband with her, and he ate." (Genesis 3:1 – 6) NKJV

In the portion of scripture above, we can clearly see that Adam and Eve used the free will they had to violate God's will. Much as Satan masterminded their disobedience and/or fall, but they could still stand their ground and refuse to listen to him. If anything, Satan did not put them at "gunpoint" that they could excuse themselves. As for me, this was just a "calculated risk". God Himself could not come in to stop them from eating the forbidden fruit because He had already commanded them not to eat or touch it. The decision that Adam and Eve took to disobey God really put their lives "at stake", and it also brought them enough consequential effects.

The effects of their consequences are still being felt up to today. The pain that women experience during childbearing and the toiling of men to earn a living are the consequences that God first gave to Adam and Eve as a result of their fall. There are many costly or fateful decisions we take which are similar to the one that Adam and Eve took, and their consequences are regrettable. Before we take any crucial decision, we should learn to reason it first and consider its benefits and shortcomings. Even if we are tempted to decide otherwise, we should reconsider it before reaching the final decision. This will help us to avoid regrets, disappointments, discouragements, humiliations and embarrassments.

CHAPTER THREE
HOW TO TEST THE VALIDITY OF A DECISION

A valid decision is the one that is logical, well based or sound. For any decision to materialize, it should therefore be valid. In this chapter of the book, I will give six elements and I trust these elements could help us to test the validity of any decision we may intend to make. These elements if not carefully observed, then our decisions will always remain invalid.

1.   FAITH:

If the basis of the decision one would like to take or has already taken is on faith, then truly his decision will be valid. There are many people who are very good at making decisions but the only missing ingredient in their decisions is faith. When challenges come, only those whose decisions are based on faith can stand the test and continue with whatever they had decided to do. Much as people could take decision to go to Jesus Christ to be healed, but He would heal them in response to their faith. In many instances, Jesus Christ said to some people after healing them "your faith has healed you".

Of all things that can please God, faith is on the lead. And without faith, it is not possible to please God. Now anything we do in faith prompts God to intervene! The Bible is very clear on faith:

> *"But without faith it is impossible to please Him: for he who comes to God must believe that He is, and that He is a rewarder of those who diligently seek Him." (Hebrews 11:6) KJV*

A person who has faith is always hopeful. Even if things are not favorable on the decision he has taken, he will remain focused still. For one to be hopeful, his hope should be backed up by the power of the Holy Spirit. This power helps him to formulate his thoughts or ideas very carefully, so that he may see what others may not and believe what could be incredible to others.

"Now may the God of hope fill you with all joy and peace in believing, that you may abound in hope by the power of the Holy Spirit." (Romans 15:13)KJV.

We may take as many right decisions as we can, but as long as we do not have faith or remain hopeful; God wouldn't be moved and in this case, He wouldn't intervene to help us especially where we need help from Him.

When I decided to begin writing books, I was aware of the likely challenges I could face since I was a first timer. First of all I didn't have enough money to publish the book. I decided therefore to ignore all the challenges that could easily force me to cowardice, and then took a step of faith and bought a rim of papers; prayed over it and I started the business. I was only eager to at least hold a copy of the book in my hand. I thank God for He intervened and provided money to publish the first book. This is my second book, even the third will soon come after this one and many more are yet to come!

2.   LOVE:
Love is another thing we may use to test the validity of our decisions. If one's basis of decision is on love, then his decision will be valid. Now God is love and His love is unconditional.

"For God so loved the world that He gave His only begotten Son, that whoever believes in Him should not perish but have everlasting life." (John 3:16) KJV

The love that God lavished upon us by sending His only begotten Son to come and save us was unconditional. He foreknew that there are those who would appreciate this love and those who would underrate it. But given the fact that His nature is love; this did not allow Him to change His mind. Those who have perfect love, they therefore have the stamina to continue to love things or people who were once lovable but have now proved to be unlovable. On the contrary, those who do not have the ability to continue to love the unlovable things or people, they may not stand this test and instead they may decide to hate them permanently!

3. ESTABLISHED TESTIMONIES:
If the basis of our decisions is on the testimonies we have established or other people's powerful testimonies, then those decisions will be valid. The testimonies we have built or other people's testimonies could help to boost our morale in making decisions. Before David in the Bible confronted and killed Goliath, he had confronted and killed many wild beasts while tending to his father's flock. So what moved David to confront Goliath among other things were his former testimonies.

The testimony I have built by writing the first book has really increased my faith. So now, as far as writing books are concerned, nothing can discourage me for I have already built a testimony. My reasoning is this, "If God could see me through in the first one, then why not this time or next time?"

Have you established testimonies or are you overwhelmed by other people's powerful testimonies? Then allow those testimonies to encourage you in making other decisions. This way, you will learn to make concrete decisions and you will stand the test in case of any eventuality that may arise.

4. MAKING COVENANTS / VOWS:
Covenants, vows, oaths or promises though some people misuse or take them for granted, but they could prove to be another test for the validity of our decisions if rightly and strictly used. The decisions we then take basing on carefully considered covenants, vows, oaths or promises, will stand the test and could last forever.

Our God is a God of covenant and His covenants are everlasting. The covenant He made between Himself and Abraham is still effective up to this present time!

"When Abram was ninety-nine years old, the Lord appeared to Abram and said to him, I am Almighty God; walk before Me and be blameless. And I will make My covenant between Me and you, and will multiply you exceedingly. Then Abram fell on his face, and God talked with him saying: As for Me, behold, My covenant is with you, and you shall be a father of many nations. No longer shall your name be called Abram, but your name shall be Abraham; for I have made you a father of many nations. I will make you exceedingly fruitful; and I will make nations of you, and kings shall come from you. And I will establish My covenant between Me and you and your descendants after you in their generations for an everlasting covenant, to be God to you and your descendants after you. Also I give to you and your descendants after you the land in which you are a stranger, all the land of Canaan, as an everlasting possession; and I will be their God. And God said to Abraham: As for you, you shall keep My covenant, you and your descendants after you throughout their generations. This is My covenant which you shall keep between Me and you and your descendants after you: Every male child among you shall be circumcised; and you shall be circumcised in the flesh of your foreskins, and it shall be a sign of the covenant between Me and you." (Genesis 17:1 - 11) NKJV

In the portion of scripture above, we can clearly see that God's basis of decision to make Abraham a father of many nations was on a covenant. A vow is another thing that could also help us to test the validity of the decisions we make.

The Bible tells us the story of Jonah how especially he was swallowed by the fish and stayed in the belly of the fish for three days and three nights, and said "He would pay what he had vowed to."

> **"But I will sacrifice to You**
> **with voice of thanksgiving;**
> **I will pay what I have vowed.**
> **Salvation is of the Lord."**
> **(Jonah 2:9) NKJV.**

The decision that Jonah made while in the belly of the fish to fulfill what he was supposed to, was based on a vow. Whenever we make a vow or a promise, we should try with our level best to fulfill it for the Bible even reminds us of the same.

> **"When you make a vow to God,**
> **do not delay to pay it; for He**
> **has no pleasure in fools. Pay**
> **what you have vowed. Better**
> **not to vow than to vow**
> **and not pay.**
> **(Ecclesiastes 5:4-5) NKJV**

The vows that the bride and the groom exchange when they are being joined in holy matrimony could prove to be a very powerful bond. And when carefully observed, this bond could maintain the married couple for the rest of their lives. On the 11th of July 2010, I exchanged vows with my wife. For I said, "I will adhere to her alone even through thick and thin till only death separate us." Now the basis of my decision to stay in the very marriage I am in till only death do us apart is on the vows I exchanged.

Therefore, what really bind me to my wife are the vows I exchanged with her for they were not just for formality. So, just as I pledged to her; I will continue to observe and fulfill my vows for as long as both of us are alive!

5. BEING WELL INFORMED:

Sometimes we may take decisions basing on the information we have got from a reliable source. Now if really the decision one would like to take is based on proven information from a reliable source, then his decision will stand the test. But if it is only based on rumors or fabricated stories, then it wouldn't stand the test.

The Bible tells us the story of Nehemiah, how especially he reacted after being reliably told about the status of the Jews who had survived the captivity.

"It came to pass in the month of Chislev, in the twentieth year, as I was in Shushan the Citadel that Hanani one of my brethren came with men from Judah; and I asked them concerning the Jews who had escaped, who had survived the captivity, and concerning Jerusalem. And they said to me, the survivors who are left from captivity in the province are there in great distress and reproach. The wall of Jerusalem is also broken down, and its gates are burned with fire. So it was, when I heard these words that I sat down and wept, and mourned for many days; I was fasting and praying before the God of heaven." (Nehemiah 1:1- 4) NKJV.

Now the decision that Nehemiah took to go and rebuild the broken wall of Jerusalem, after praying and fasting to God for counsel; was based on the information he had got. Since it was a true report, Nehemiah went and saw the dilapidated state of Jerusalem's wall and its gates just as he had been told.

6. THE DIVINE PERFECT WILL OF GOD:

The decision we take basing on the divine will or plan of God are always valid and those decisions could stand the test when trial moments come. The Bible says, **"Plans are established by counsel; and by wise counsel wage war."** Now those who have learnt the secret of taking decisions that are based on God's divine will or plan, their decisions will never flop.

Now the question is, "how could we take decisions that are based on God's will?" The answer is simple; we could either use logo or remah words of God. The logo are God's words written in His Holy book, whereas Rhema are those words we get by revelation or as a result of inquiring of God. Sometimes we may receive those words as prophesy. The Bible narrates King David's habitual mentality of making inquiries from God. One incident that prompted David to inquire of the Lord was the Amalekites' invasion that left him and his men without wives, children, properties and the entire city vandalized!

"Now it happened, when David and his men came to Ziklag, on the third day, that the Amalekites had invaded the South and Ziklag, attacked Ziklag and burned it with fire, and had taken captive the women and those who were there, from small to great; they did not kill anyone, but carried them away and went their way. So David and his men came to the city, and there it was burned with fire; and their wives, their sons, and their daughters had been taken captive. Then David and the people who were with him lifted up their voices and wept, until they had no more power to weep. And David's two wives, Ahinoam the Jezreelitess and Abigail the widow of Nabal the Carmelite, had been taken captive. Now David was greatly distressed, for the people spoke of stoning him, because the soul of all the people was grieved, every man for his sons and his daughters. But David strengthened himself in the Lord his God. Then David said to Abiathar the priest, Ahimelech's son, please bring the ephod here to me. And Abiathar brought the ephod to David. So David inquired of the Lord, saying, shall I pursue this troop? Shall I overtake them? And He answered him, pursue, for you shall surely overtake them and without fail recover all." (1 Samuel 30: 1 -8) NKJV

In the verses above, it is clear that the decision that David took to pursue the Amalekites was based on God's will and the result was great. David together with his men recovered all that the Amalekites had taken, lacking nothing of theirs which they had lost!

When God told me to stop teaching in order to serve Him, to marry the wife I am with now and to begin writing books; I obeyed and I made decisions based on His will. The results are now enjoyable and I am tuned in to the next thing He will tell me to do and I will be right to it.

Has God told you to do something? Do not delay, just obey Him and base your decisions on His will. Though challenges could be threatening to tear your faith or hope, just take courage for His grace is sufficient on you and enormous rewards await!

CHAPTER FOUR
WHEN DO WE MAKE A DECISION?

Day-to-day life is characterized by decision- making, and our daily lives are driven by the decisions we make. The decisions we make are what order or control our actions or programs. So, whatever we shall decide to do any particular day, will determine how we shall end that day. When we decide to do or not to do, then our achievements or failures for that particular day will be as a result of the decisions we shall have then made.

Now depending on the intensity or urgency of any given situation or problem in question, we may take decisions now or later. There are some decisions we take intuitively on a daily basis without other people necessarily telling us to make them. When for instance someone is famished and very ready to eat or when he has a call of nature, he wouldn't need another person to tell him to respond to those demands.

The decisions we take to respond to the demands mentioned above are driven by the in-born feelings that come out automatically. There are some matters that are simple and they only require us to use permissive or the free will God has given us to decide on them.

But a matter of the greatest urgency demands prompt actions. If for example someone has involved himself in a fatal accident that has left him in a critical condition, we should with everything within our means devise a quicker way of coming to his rescue.
There are many other matters similar to the one mentioned above, that are really of urgency and they yet call for immediate decisions. If really we should handle any matter of urgency, then we should avoid procrastination and not being decisive. For those who always procrastinate or are not decisive cannot handle any matter of this nature.

There are some matters that require crucial decisions. And when handling them, we should first give careful thoughts before reaching the final decision. Sometimes we have to consider and reconsider our decisions before coming out with the final ones. It is even advisable to test the validity of the decision we intend to make as given in chapter three of this book.

So for any sensitive matter, we should be extra careful lest we make fateful decisions whose effects would then be felt on our future. We should not rush into making final decisions while handling matters of this sort, but rather take sometime to seek counsel and pray to God and then come out with our final decisions.

The Bible says, **"So then, my beloved brethren, let every man be swift to hear, slow to speak, slow to wrath." (James 1:19) KJV**

According to this portion of scripture given, we may not react to everything we have heard there and then. Sometimes people may speak bad things about us which are not true in reality, just in the interest of tarnishing our reputations. In this case, how would you react? If you have a clear conscience about your innocence on the said allegations, just leave the battle to the Lord. One day your innocence shall be established and all your enemies will be ashamed before your very eyes. Do not then decide to react badly. For any decision we take in wrath will obviously breed another problem. And besides, a man's wrath does not produce God's righteousness.

If they have spoken ill about you, do not decide to pay back evil with evil. Consider forgiving them first even as you seek God's wisdom to handle the matter.

CHAPTER FIVE
HOW TO DEAL WITH ORDEALS

Ordeals are those difficult or painful moments we do experience in our lives. And those moments really test our characters or abilities to endure those difficulties we are always faced with. Ordeals are common phenomena that everyone goes through in life. It is vital to know that ordeals come for different reasons. Sometimes they come as a result of our own mistakes or others' mistakes, and in most cases they happen naturally but with God's or Satan's finger on them. Now regardless of how they come, but their effects are the same on us. People's ordeals most commonly and readily come in the following areas: Frequent persecutions, frequent disasters or misfortunes, loss of jobs, loss of dear ones , loss of properties or valuables, deferred hopes, unanswered prayers, oppressions; divorce or broken relationships, unbecoming situations, constraints, sexual abuses or molestations, barrenness or impotence, persistent sicknesses, un-repented sins and failures in general.

It is yet important to know that ordeals are inevitable and in vast majority of cases, they come unexpectedly. Since they are decisive moments, then it would require carefully considered decisions to handle them. For when one fails to make a wise decision while in a difficult moment, then his situation might go from bad to worse. Indeed some people's root causes of their poor health are as a result of the ordeals they do experience. This is so because when one is overwhelmed by pains or is frantic with fear, worries, anger and bitterness; he could easily get psychological torture resulting sometimes in strain, stress, stroke and insanity.

Others might also get hypertension, heart disease and abnormal loss of weight. The worst bit of it is that some people consider committing suicide after especially coming to the end of themselves! We should then be very careful on where to base our decisions whenever we are in ordeal moment.

What we stand for matters a lot when it comes to making decisions in ordeal moments. Those who trust in their own ability or wisdom may rely on them when faced with difficult moments. Those who believe and trust in Satan may consider seeking those who are mediums for solutions to their ordeals, or applying witchcraft to get solutions to their problems. And those who believe and trust in God may decide to cry to Him for mercy and solutions to their ordeals.

But as for me, I would suggest that we handle our ordeals while considering their causes. When for instance one is suffering because of his mistakes or sins, he should then correct his mistakes and avoid repeating them or repent genuinely and forsake those sins. It's also advisable to always discard our past mistakes or sins, and make a fresh start to avoid suffering the torments of remorse for a long time. But even so, it's worthwhile knowing that some people may continue to identify us with the past mistakes or sins we committed even a decade ago! This should not in any way discourage us for that is according to man.

But as for the Lord God, He forgives our sins, removes them far away and remembers them no more! For it is written, **"As far as the east is from the west, so far has He removed our transgressions from us."** **(Psalm 103:12) KJV**

When our ordeals are because of others' mistakes or sins, it's advisable to repent still on their behalf; pleading with God to forgive them, and from the bottom of our hearts we should forgive them and remain at peace with them. Though it is not easy to forgive our afflicters, persecutors or those who have wronged us; but we have no better choice than forgiveness as long as we want to have no trouble with God and to remain peaceful. For when we fail to forgive, then it will by all means hinder our prayers, breakthroughs and blessings from God!

The Bible is crystal clear on this. For it's written; **"For whenever you stand praying, if you have anything against anyone, forgive him that your Father in heaven may also forgive you your trespasses. But if you do not forgive, neither will your Father in heaven forgive you your trespasses."(Mark 11: 25 - 26) NKJV**

From the portion of scripture above, it's clear that unforgiveness hinders our prayers. And once our prayers are hindered, then our deliverance or breakthroughs shall also be delayed. So then, when one wants to stay longer in the ordeals brought by others; let him simply not forgive and the reverse is true. So the choice is ours.

When after examining ourselves and we discover that our walks with the Lord are perfect, without even being suspicious of other people as the causers of our ordeals; then it could be certain that these particular ordeals have naturally come. Now the best way to handle ordeals of this kind is to first of all repent regardless of whether we have sinned or not. Afterwards we should then prayerfully discover whether it's Satan's finger or God's finger that we suffer. For when it's Satan's ugly finger, then we should with all sorts of prayers wage war against him. It's vital to know that by the virtue of the authority given to us and in Jesus' name, we have a clear mandate to bind and cast out demons or wicked spirits responsible for our afflictions or sufferings.

But when it's God's finger, we should pour out our hearts to Him with all sorts of prayers pleading for mercy. Since He's a faithful God, then He wouldn't fail to grant answers to our petitions. Even if He delays we shouldn't be discouraged, for delay is not denial. At His own appointed time - He will for sure see us through! In fact God is the only One who can heal our wounds and broken hearts – for He is our Father and creator.

In the Bible, we are told of those who went through difficult moments and how they handled them. In the book of second kings, we are told the story of the four lepers who really had a chastening experience and the decision they took that bailed them out.

"Now there were four leprous men at the entrance of the gate; and they said to one another, why are we sitting here until we die? If we say, we will enter the city, the famine is in the city, and we shall die there. And if we sit here, we die also. Now therefore, come, let us surrender to the army of the Syrians. If they keep us alive, we shall live; and if they kill us, we shall only die. And they arose at twilight to go to the camp of Syrians; and when they had come to the outskirts of the Syrians camp, to their surprise no one was there .For the Lord had caused the army of Syrians to hear the noise of chariots and the noise of horses- the noise of a great army; so they said to one another, look, the king of Israel has hired against us the kings of the Hittites and the kings of Egyptians to attack us! Therefore they arose and fled at twilight, and left the camp intact- their tents, their horses, and their donkeys- and they fled for their lives.

And when these lepers came to the outskirts of the camp, they went into one tent and ate and drank, and carried from it silver and gold and clothing, and went and hid them; then they came back and entered another tent, and carried some from there also, and went and hid it." (2 kings 7: 3 -8) NKJV

In the old testament of the Bible, the lepers were regarded as outcasts or ritually uncleaned people. So they were not allowed to stay or mix themselves with those who were ritually cleaned. In the portion of scripture above, the four lepers made a right choice and that was how they survived starving to death! They acted in faith and wisdom and God was on their side. God was fully aware of their situation but He only came in after they had taken a decision and a step of faith! Here we can learn that whenever we are in a situation similar to this one, we should take positive actions rather than waiting to be engulfed in it.

In the Bible, we are also told of Joseph who really went through difficult moments and how he finally came out of them all. Joseph's ordeals started when his brothers stripped him of his tunic, then took him and cast him into a pit: and then sold him to the Ishmaelite's, who later took him down to Egypt and again sold him to Potiphar, who was an officer and captain of the guard of king Pharaoh.

The most tragic moment in Joseph's life was his imprisonment that came after Potiphar's wife had allegedly reported him of attempting to rape her.

"And it came to pass after these things that his master's wife cast longing eyes on Joseph, and she said, lie with me. But he refused and said to his master's wife look, my master does not know what is with me in the house, and he has committed all that he has to my hand. There is no one greater in this house than I, nor has he kept back anything from me but you, because you are his wife. How then could I do this great wickedness, and sin against God? So it was as she spoke to Joseph day by day, that he did not heed her, to lie with her or to be with her. But it happened about this time, when Joseph went into the house to do his work, and none of the men of the house was inside, that she caught him by his garment, saying, lie with me. But he left his garment in her hand, and fled and ran outside that she called to the men of her house and spoke to them saying, see he has brought in to us a Hebrew to mock us. He came into me to lie with me, and I cried out with a loud voice.

And it happened, when he heard that I lifted my voice and cried that he left his garment with me, and fled and went outside. So she kept his garment with her until his master came home. Then she spoke to him with words like these, saying, the Hebrew servant whom you brought to us came into me to mock me; so it happened as I lifted my voice and cried out, that he left his garment with me and fled outside.

So it was when his master heard the words which his wife spoke to him, saying your servant did to me after this manner, that his anger was aroused. Then Joseph's master took him and put him into the prison, a place where the king's prisoners were confined. And he was there in the prison." (Genesis 39: 7-20) NKJV

In chapter 41 of the book of Genesis, we are told how Joseph interpreted Pharaoh's dreams and then rose to power. This was how Joseph ended his ordeals for he was removed from prison to an office. Joseph's breakthrough was different from that of the four lepers; for his was the wisdom he had that brought his breakthrough and he did not struggle to get his breakthrough! Sometimes when we are in a difficult moment, the very "intrinsic worth" we have inside us is what we may use to get a breakthrough!

God has deposited in everyone some packages of gifts and talents, but because of ignorance we may suffer for a long time especially with financial problem as long as we are not making the best use of those gifts or talents to obtain money. There are many people who are in ordeal of financial constraint and yet inside them there are many undiscovered gifts and talents which are just intact!

The Bible says, **"A man's gift makes room for him, and brings him before great men." (Proverbs 18:16).** The Ugandan 2012 golden Olympic hero, "Stephen Kiprotich," is a man who discovered his talent and started to develop, nurture and cultivate it till it produced him before great men! The victory this young man got because of his talent has made a tremendous impact on his life now and forever.

Before I discovered myself as a writer, the gift was just intact and I had never thought of one day becoming a writer! I may not be such a good or an influential writer, but one thing I know, I have discovered it as a gift that was inside me and I have seriously started to develop, nurture and cultivate it.

Are you in ordeal moment? Do not allow it to rob you of your faith, hope, courage, love, patience and confidence. Sometimes the problem may appear big for nothing. For when we decide to take actions in faith, the problem will for sure depart from us. When the Israelites were faced with one of the most challenging ordeal moments, God told Moses to just use the rod he was holding in his hand to solve the problem! For the Lord said to Moses, "lift your rod and stretch your hand over the sea in order to divide it." Imagine how burdened the Israelites were, for the Egyptians were pursuing them and yet right before them, the Red Sea had stood as the greatest obstacle!

I guess some of the Israelites in their turmoil considered surrendering to the Egyptian troops, others probably spoke of stoning Moses and some may be thought of diving into the sea. **(See the book of Exodus and read the all of chapter fourteen).**

Whenever we are in a decisive moment, we should avoid "Plan B" or short cuts for they may only help us momentarily. God has also promised that He will be with us always in both good and bad times and from a distance He watches over us. We should then stop coming to God as a last resort but rather give Him the first place for He cares for us. The Bible encourages us to be of good courage even in hard moments for God is ever watchful.

"But now, thus says the Lord, who created you, O Jacob, and He who formed you, O Israel: fear not for I have redeemed you; I have called you by your name; you are Mine. When you pass through the waters, I will be with you. When you walk through the fire, you shall not be burned, nor shall the flame scorch you. For I am the Lord your God, the Holy One of Israel, Your Savior, I gave Egypt for your ransom, Ethiopia and Seba in your place."(Isaiah 43: 1 – 3) NKJV

Though chastening experiences are painful and unpleasant to us, but God takes advantage of them to glorify His name and to mould and make us what He wants us to be. So then, the decisions we take when we are in hard times should allow the will of God to be done in us, for it will yield the fruit of righteousness!

"Now no chastening seems to be joyful for the present, but painful, nevertheless, afterward, it yields the peaceable fruit of righteousness to those who have been trained by it. Therefore strengthen the hands which hang down, and the feeble knees, and make straight paths for your feet. So that what is lame may not be dislocated but rather be healed." (Hebrews 12: 11 – 13) KJV

Sometimes God allows painful or unpleasant moments to befall us so that we may build His godly characters to help us walk uprightly before Him. To those who are not patient, God may delay to answer them so that they may build the character of patience. To the fearful, God may allow a very frightening situation or problem to face them so that they may build the character of boldness. To those who are in complacent state, God may allow a very challenging situation to come on their ways just in the interest of creating awareness and awakening in them; and this will definitely force them to get out of their comfort zones and they will for sure begin to seek Him by offering serious prayers, thus drawing them nearer to Him. And in most cases God uses unpleasant situations to test our faith. James in the Bible in his book encourages us to count it all joy when faced with unbecoming situations.

For its written, ***"My brethren count it all joy when you fall into various trials, knowing that the testing of your faith produces patience. But let patience have its perfect work, that you may be perfect lacking nothing."(James 1: 2- 4) KJV***

Instead of being mad with God when we are in ordeal moments, we should learn to humble ourselves before Him in prayers seeking for His mercy lest we become profane and we hinder His will to be done in us. We should stop treating God as an enemy and we begin to see Him as a deliverer. There is a saying that goes like "Every why has a wherefore," meaning things do not just happen without a reason. So now, unless we know the "whys" of our ordeals, we should stop reacting madly.

As for the Lord God, He wants us to be thankful even when faced with difficulties. For it's written, **"In everything give thanks; for this is the will of God in Christ Jesus for you."(1 Thessalonians 5: 18) KJV**

Since it's God's will that we thank Him in everything, we should then always do His will by being thankful even in unpleasant moments. The verses in Romans 8: 28 comfort us with these words, "***And we know that all things work together for good to those who love God to those who are called according to His purpose.***" So then, we should always encourage ourselves that even bad things work for good and that is when we shall always be at peace and not even moved.

It is very vital to know that sometimes God Himself allows Satan to inflict problems on us, just in the interest of testing us in the areas of love, patience, faith or character. This kind of experience is what none wants to go through for in most cases, it lasts longer and as long as we are in it, life seems to be empty. Now this kind of ordeal does not necessarily come because we have sinned, but rather because God wants to test us. As a case in point, Job in the Bible had a taste of this kind of experience. Much as Job was a righteous man before God, but it came to pass that calamities befell him--- and which calamities left him without children, possessions and with painful boils!

"Now there was a day when the sons of God came to present themselves before the Lord, and Satan also came among them. And the Lord said to Satan, "From where do you come?"

So Satan answered the Lord and said, "From going to and fro on the earth, and from walking back and forth on it". Then the Lord said to Satan, "Have you considered My servant Job, that there is none like him on the earth, a blameless and upright man, who fears God and shuns evil?"

So Satan answered the Lord and said, "Does Job fear God for nothing? Have You not made a hedge around him, around his household, and around all that he has on every side? You have blessed the work of his hands, and his possessions have increased in the land. But now stretch out Your hand and touch all that he has, and he will surely curse You to Your face!" and the Lord said to Satan, "behold, all that he has is in your power; only do not lay a hand on his person". So Satan went from the presence of the Lord. Now there was a day when his sons and daughters were eating and drinking wine in their oldest brother's house; and a messenger came to Job and said, "The oxen were ploughing and the donkeys feeding beside them, when the Sabeans raided them away – indeed they have killed the servants with the edge of the sword; and I alone have escaped to tell you!" while he was still speaking, another also came and said, "

The fire of God fell from heavens and burned up the sheep and the servants, and consumed them; and I alone have escaped to tell you!" While he was still speaking, another also came and said, "The Chaldeans formed three bands, raided the camels and took them away, yes, and killed the servants with the edge of the sword; and I alone have escaped to tell you!" While he was still speaking, another also came and said, "Your sons and daughters were eating and drinking wine in their oldest brother's house, and suddenly a great wind came from across the wilderness and struck the four corners of the house, and it fell on the young people, and they are dead; and I alone have escaped to tell you!" (Job 1:6-20)NKJV

In the previous verses, it is clear that God allowed Satan to test Job's character. But even in this painful experience, Job chose to praise God and to remain in good relationship with Him. Job is then the best role model as far as dealing with ordeal of this nature is concerned. So then, when one is in this kind of ordeal, he should learn to copy Job's example. Now one could ask himself this question, "How could I know that this kind of awful experience I am in is because of Satan's infliction though on God's permission?" The answer is simple, when after offering all sorts of prayers, while believing in God as well and even being in position to justify your walks before the Lord; and all these attempts seem to be giving no remedy, and yet you have been in this kind of experience for quite long, then do not hesitate to conclude that God has connived with Satan to test you!

In most cases when one is in this kind of experience, other people might quickly conclude that it is because of sin that he suffers. So it is advisable that the affected person blames nobody not even God or Satan though he might have suffered for a long time. He should only maintain good relationship with God and with unceasing prayers he should continue to trust in the Lord for a breakthrough. For one day when God is done with him, He will remember him and divinely visit him and change his tears to laughter, sorrows to joy and sufferings to celebration! It will them come to pass that some of those who knew him before will begin to testify of his divine visitation on his behalf and to others it will bring salvation yet to others amazement and shame.

CHAPTER SIX
THE BEST WAY TO ENTER INTO MARRIAGE

Marriage is a very precious thing that is morally or legally acceptable in every society of the nations of the world. Since it's precious, we should then handle it with care. Now God Himself is the author of marriage, for He first instituted it in the Garden of Eden when He created Adam and Eve respectively as husband and wife. When God saw that it was not good for Adam to stay alone, He caused a deep sleep to fall on him and removed one of his ribs and made it into a woman. It was very possible for God to create Eve without necessarily removing one of Adam's ribs, but what I perceive here is that, God considered certain things since it was the first marriage. By the virtue of Adam being created first, God wanted him to remain the head of the family. When He removed one of the ribs of Adam and created it into a woman, I understand He wanted to establish a strong bond in this couple to become one flesh, stay in harmony and to have mutual understanding.

No wonder, when Adam woke up from sleep he spoke these words: **"This is now bone of my bones and flesh of my flesh; she shall be called woman because she was taken out of man. Therefore a man shall leave his father and mother and be joined to his wife and they shall become one flesh." (Genesis 2:23 – 24) NKJV**

So, considering God's set-up in the first marriage, we should then take decisions to enter into marriage while observing the basic things in this set-up. One's decision to enter into marriage should therefore help them get a partner to stay with in harmony and mutual understanding without any struggle or neglect of position and everyone playing his or her role effectively.

It is important to know that entering into marriage is like signing one's life away. So whoever wants to enter into it should consider certain things, before deciding to commit them in that particular marriage. One could first ask themselves these vital questions; Am I ready to remain a man or a woman in this marriage I would like to enter into? Am I ready to be joined as one flesh with my spouse? Will I treat my wife as a property or as a gift from God? Will I love my wife as a man or will I submit to my husband as a woman? Will I defend the marriage I would like to enter into as a woman or a man throughout my life? Won't I give in – in case I encounter challenges in future? Will this marriage in the very way I would like to enter into give glory to God or it will instead destroy His glory?

Many people have different views when it comes to marriage. Some may consider the following things: One's level of education, nationality / tribe, background, age, health status, marital status, financial status, religion, tradition, culture, norms, customs, beauty / stature or size, sexuality and conduct / character or behavior.

Others may consider all the features given above and yet rely on other people for making choice or decision. There are those who may consider just some of the features given above and still rely on others for decision making or choice. And there are some who may only consider some of the features given above and trust in God still for wise counsel leading them to ideal partners!

In some rare cases, some people only take their marriage partners at their face values without bothering to consider other things. They use the principle of "first sight first love". Some people who fall in this category also trust in God for counsel and provision after coming to agreement with the "would–be marriage partner".

The different views that people have or the things they consider while entering into marriage are all about the preparations of the heart. The Bible says, **"The preparations of the heart belong to man, but the answer of the tongue is from the Lord." (Proverbs 16:1) KJV.**

How one has prepared his or her heart will then determine the things he or she will allow in the heart or mind. And the things one has permitted in his or her heart / mind will affect his or her decisions positively or negatively! Some people who do not want to marry or delay to marry is because of lack of preparations of the heart. For their perceptions about marriage is completely different from what God has planned for them! Those who have prepared their hearts to only taking things in "Silver plate," may not accept the proposals of those whom they consider unqualified, though they could be ideal ones from God! In some exceptional cases, God draws people together in marriage so that His purposes may be fulfilled in them. This may only happen to those who have prepared their hearts, and are ready to say "Let your will be done oh Lord."

Now regardless of our views about marriage, or how prepared or unprepared we are in our hearts; so long as we have decided to marry or to be married to someone, what matters is how to begin the process. Some people after engagement begin to cohabit straightaway. Others consider going for introduction and paying the dowry first then they begin to stay together. And there are those who even after paying the dowry, would still not want to defile themselves till they enter into the holy state of marriage.

According to God's principles concerning marriage, the last category mentioned above is highly recommended. The Bible in the book of Hebrews 13:14 gives a serious warning against fornicators and adulterers for it's written, **"Marriage is honorable among all, and the bed undefiled; but fornicators and adulterers God will judge."**

So then, the only befitting way of entering into marriage is the godly one, for it brings favour and blessings from God. If God's glory is to be manifested in our marriages, then we should go the godly way, and this portion of scripture that says **"he who finds a wife finds a good thing and obtains favor from the Lord,"** will then immediately and effectively begin to work in our marriages.

So, those who have entered into marriage while not observing God's principles; He regards them as fornicators, not until they make up their minds to sanctify their marriages by being joined in holy matrimony. But for those who indulge themselves in this kind of practice after knowing the truth or accepting Jesus Christ as their Lord and savior, God handles them in a different way for He is not mocked. Much as he may forgive them after they have sanctified their marriages, but the consequences may endure for as long as the victims are together in that particular marriage!

The Bible says, **"If the foundations are destroyed what can the righteous do?**" The basis of a foundation therefore matters a lot. For when one's foundation of marriage is based on fornication, then it will call for judgement as clearly stipulated in the Bible. If the foundation is based on beauty or material things, when beauty or material things disappear; then the marriage will also disappear. If the foundation is based on God's principles, then in case of any challenge He will be the most immediate person to turn to.

It's vital to know that both God and Satan are interested in the foundation of everything. If one's foundation of marriage is based on the things that could give glory to God, then the future of his marriage will remain in God's hands for He has legal ground in it. But if the foundation of one's marriage is based on the things that could give glory to Satan, then this will attract him to have full control over his marriage for he has legal ground to enter.

My general counsels to whoever wants to enter into marriage are these: After getting your marriage partner, inform your spiritual leaders about it. Let your parents, close relatives and friends in whom you confide also be informed. Since Satan is not pleased with those who want to fulfill God's righteousness, he may try to fight the marriage with the aims of either breaking it or causing the couple to fall into fornication so that he takes the glory. It is then advisable to begin serious prayers to cancel every wicked schemes of Satan and above all, refuse totally to defile yourself before officially being joined in holy matrimony as husband and wife. As long as you have loved each other, turn a deaf ear to people's words of discouragement and jealously.

Together with the Church leaders, plan and arrange for the things that are required of you.

If one of you decides to give up for the reason best known to him or her, you who is focused try to win him or her back prayerfully. When he or she refuses completely even after the Church leaders' and other people's counsels, leave him or her alone for if his or her decision was based on genuine love then you will finally stay together. But if not, then do not try to force someone who does not love you to marry you. For those who may succeed in entering into the holy state of marriage after everything is sorted, they should not relax even after the wedding for Satan does not easily give up. Get ready to defend your marriage from day one till you depart this life. How could one defend his or her marriage?

It's simple, he should offer to God unceasing prayers to protect the foundation of his marriage. Another thing which is also very vital to observe is the renewal of the marriage covenants. The covenants, vows of promises that the couple exchange before and during the time they are being joined in holy matrimony could be the best way to consolidate marital relationships.

So, the best way to defend one's marriage is to renew the covenants, vows or promises they exchanged on their wedding day over and over again. It's advisable to make it a daily routine to renew the following things that the couples do pledge to each other that is: love, trust, care, honor, submission, sincerity, patience, faithfulness or fidelity and mutuality.

Do not allow anything to destroy your marriage. Challenges or difficult moments will always come even as you continue with your marital journey, but always remain as one and fight a common goal for the betterment of your marriage. The decisions we therefore take when preparing to enter into marriage should also help us to remain firm forever in our marriages.

Another thing to take note of is that, when you feel it is lust of the flesh driving you to marriage, and then first overcome it before entering into it. For if not, you will enter into marriage lustfully and even continue to lust after other men or women. Now cheating on your spouse is a very disgraceful thing that could easily lead to divorce.

So it is advisable to first not enter into marriage before dealing with our lustful sexual desires. Why then should a married man or woman commit adultery? Isn't this lust of the flesh? Those who therefore have high appetite for sex have lust of the flesh, some of this category of people may commit the sins of incest, bestiality, and others may defile their own daughters!

CHAPTER SEVEN
DO YOU WANT TO BE AN OVERCOMER?

In the arena of human life, there are many people who are overcome by many things. And those things they are overcome with are masters over their lives. So as many as are overcome by certain things, these are ones enslaved to those things they are overcome with. Therefore if we should overcome the things we are overcome with, we have to take serious decisions.

It's vital to know that to be overcome is to be overpowered. So if we should overcome, we *ought* to overpower. But overpowering does not work for everybody except for those who are tired or are fed up with those things they are enslaved to and are ready to say enough is enough; those who are ready for "do or die actions", those who are desperate for a change in their lives and are ready to fight till they gain control over the things they are overcome with, and those who are ready to reorganize their lives so that even after overpowering their "masters," they will continue to be on offensive to avoid being overcome again.

Though people are overcome differently, but at least in some of these areas they are overcome: emotions, power of Satan, sin, problems, situations, circumstances, habits and addicts. Now as long as we are still enslaved to something, then we shall continue to subject to it. For a slave's duty is to obey the master. Whatever his master tells him he ought to obey.

Those who are overcome by any sin, they should take tough decisions to conquer it. Reason it this way, sin takes people to hell, so why should I die in sin and go to hell? Begin to avoid and hate it, stop it once and for all and renounce it forthwith. On a serious note, just decide to refuse to commit that particular sin and the sin will shy away from you!

One sin that has eaten up the body of Christ and has greatly overcome its victims is that of sexual immorality. This is one sin that defiles one's body which is God's temple and Satan being well aware of it, lures many to commit it.

Sexual immorality is one sin we shouldn't play around with, for it is very easy to commit it and yet very difficult to overcome. Nevertheless, it is very possible to overcome sexual immorality. For if one does not demand sex from another, or if one does not succumb to another's sexual demand then they wouldn't commit it.

In the Bible, we are told of Job's serious decision of overcoming sexual immorality, for he said; "***I have made a covenant with my eyes, why then should I look upon a young woman lustfully?" (Job 31:1).*** Job was a righteous man before God, but he had still to take a serious decision to overcome sexual immorality. I also took a serious decision to overcome sexual immorality, and now my confessions are these; "may God strike me to death on the spot when I commit it, and let there also be writings all over my body parts saying: his death is as a result of sexual immorality, and on seeing it, let no one bother to burry me." It may sound ridiculous, but as for me, that is my stand as far as overcoming sexual immorality is concerned!

Another thing that also bothers many people to overcome is poverty. The level of poverty varies from one person to another, and there are many and different reasons why some people are poor. One most common reason why some people are poor is the "mind–set" about poverty.

This mind–set makes them reason as poor people, behave like poor people, look like poor people and they also careless about their creature comforts! So the genesis of overcoming poverty is the change of mind-set about it. There are many people who are financially stable - with even plenty of material things, but they still look poor because of their poverty mentalities. This category of people is not gifted in giving neither do they want others to know that they are well of. Some rich people even put their families on strict diet!

As for me, though I do not have enough money as yet to acquire the things I am in need of, but I do not behave like a poor man, neither do I entertain poverty. I am on a serious campaign of "kick poverty out of my life". When one really hates something, they wouldn't want to identify themselves with that particular thing. I have decided to fight poverty till I overcome it completely. It is not enough to just pray or to be prayed for to get financial breakthrough, for prosperity begins with a positive mind–set. For as a man thinks, so is he and as he confesses, so he will become.

Another thing that many people do battle with to overcome is the power of Satan. Truly, many people are afflicted and oppressed by Satan's power and they are helplessly stranded! Satan's power manifests in us for two reasons: It could either be because we fellowship with unfruitful works of darkness like witchcraft and/or sorcery, sexual immorality, idolatry, speaking lies just to mention but a few; or Satan himself for the reason of subjecting us to sufferings and bondages.

If we should overcome Satan's power, we have to take uncompromising decisions to fight it till we are delivered. This strategy may only work for those who are not ready to fellowship with unfruitful works of darkness as mentioned above, and are also fully attached to God's Kingdom. For as long as someone is still in the camp of Satan, then it wouldn't be easy for him to overcome the power of this Kingdom he belongs to.

So if we should overcome Satan's power, we have to first come out of his camp and then be fully attached to God's Kingdom and then begin to push back his power with a very aggressive spiritual warfare weapons. So the choice is ours. For we may choose to come out of Satan's Kingdom and be fully attached to God's Kingdom, and begin to pray and get delivered from his power or we may choose to remain in his kingdom and continue to be oppressed and afflicted.

Other things which have also overcome some people are bad habits and addicts. In point of fact, there are people in this life with bad habits and others who are addicted to certain things. So for these categories of people to overcome their bad habits or whatever they are addicted to, they should first come to their senses and then they realize the dangers of those things. For someone to overcome like smoking, he should on a serious note make a "virtue of necessity" and once and for all give up with it.

It should then be our earnest prayers and desperate yearnings to overcome those things which have overcome us, for they are enmities to our breakthroughs and they could cause delay for God's purposes to be fulfilled in us!

CHAPTER EIGHT
HOW TO REGISTER SUCCESS

Success begins with a positive thinking and a positive outlook on life. Those who therefore think positively or look at life positively are the ones who may succeed in life. When God is beginning on something or when He is raising up somebody, He looks at that thing or person as a finished product! So if we may imitate God, we should then begin looking at those things we are planning to do as finished products already.

Though there could be many impediments standing in the doorway of your success, just decide to overlook them and only focus on the result. If really we should register any success, then it would require the following things:

1. PASSION:
Passion is that strong spirit of determination that cannot be stopped. So then, only passionate people may succeed in life or in their pursuits. Though success may seem to be empty in the beginning, but to those who are prone to success that calls for no alarm; for the determination they have keeps them focused and pressing on.

In the Bible, we are told the story of the proposed plan and the building of the "Tower of Babel."

"Now the whole earth had one language and one speech. And it came to pass, as they journeyed from the east that they dwelt there. Then they said to one another, come, let us make bricks and bake them thoroughly. They had brick for stone, and they had asphalt for mortar.

And they said, come, let us build ourselves a city, and a tower whose top is in the heavens; let us make a name for ourselves, lest we be scattered abroad over the face of the whole earth. But the Lord came down to see the city and the tower which the son of men had built.

And the Lord said, indeed the people are one and they all have one language, and this is what they begin to do; now nothing that they propose to do will be withheld from them. Come let us go down and there confuse their language, that they may not understand one another's speech. So the Lord scattered them abroad from there over the face of all the earth, and they ceased building the city. Therefore its name is called Babel, because there the Lord confused the language of all the earth; and from there the Lord scattered them abroad over the face of all the earth." (Genesis 11: 1 – 9) NKJV

In the previous scripture, we can clearly see how determined these people were, and which determination moved God to come down and confuse their language since they had only one language and one speech! For God said in verse six, "indeed the people are one and they all have one language, and this is what they begin to do; now nothing that they propose to do will be withheld from them." Satan hates those who are determined or are passionate for doing good things for they are a threat to him.
But as for the Lord God, He likes them and He holds them with high esteem. So, it takes the spirit of determination for someone to succeed in doing good or evil.

2. ENDURANCE:
Endurance, longsuffering, perseverance and patience are of great importance when one wants to become successful in anything. If we should succeed then we have to be clothed with the Spirit of endurance. Sometimes we succeed after going through several difficulties for a long time. So in this case, only those who have the ability to endure challenges may continue with their decisions and succeed thereafter.

The Bible urges us to have endurance for it is written, **"For you have need of endurance, so that after you have done the will of God, you may receive the promise." (Hebrews 10:36) KJV.** God has promised many things to us, but it will take endurance for us to receive those promises.

God is perfect patience, so for us to succeed we should imitate Him, for God Himself endures us patiently till we come to true repentance.

"The Lord is not slack concerning His promise, as some count slackness, but is long- suffering toward us, not willing that we should perish but that all should come to repentance." (2 Peter 3: 9) KJV.

If we therefore want to succeed in becoming partakers of God's promise concerning the second coming of Jesus Christ, we should then continue waiting patiently and eagerly till He comes.

3. PERSISTENCE:
Persistence is also of necessity if we want to become successful in our doings or pursuits. Sometimes we may not be successful in the first or even second attempts, but this should not cause us to give up; we should instead continue persistently till we succeed. The only thing we should do is to keep on changing strategies and approaches each time we attempt till we succeed in our pursuits. Satan does not easily give up on God's children, why then should we as God's children give up easily while in pursuit of something?

The Bible tells us a parable that Jesus Christ gave concerning persistence:

"Then He spoke a parable to them, that men always ought to pray and not to lose heart, saying; there was in a certain city a judge who did not fear God nor regard man. Now there was a widow in that city; and she came to him, saying, get justice for me from my adversary.

"And he would not for a while; but afterward he said within himself, though I do not fear God nor regard man, yet because this widow troubles me I will avenge her, lest by her continual coming she weary me." (Luke 18: 1 – 5) KJV

In the portion of scripture above, we can notice that persistence made the widow to get justice for her adversary. This widow persisted till the judge who did not even fear God nor regard man avenged for her. So whenever we decide to pray or to do something, we should persist until something happens. We shouldn't give up until the battle is over. For where there is resistance, there must be persistence in order to overcome that resistance.

4. VISIONS:

Visions or dreams are very necessary if we should succeed, for they are goals we set before us to be achieved. Though true visionaries are often misunderstood by their own generation, but they are successful people in life. Some visions or dreams are too big that may not be handled by the bearers alone. So they have to envision others to help them fulfill their visions or dreams. Therefore unless we have visions or dreams, then our pursuits will avail nothing. The Bible says, **"Where there is no revelation, the people cast off restraint; but happy is he who keeps the law." (Proverbs 29:18) KJV**

So for us to become successful, we should have visions or dreams to pursue. And any vision or dream we have, we shouldn't let it go but rather treasure with much diligence till it comes to pass.

5. SACRIFICE:
Success goes together with sacrifice, and only those who are ready to sacrifice themselves or anything within their means may succeed in whatever they intend to do. Even God had to sacrifice His only begotten Son to die for mankind, so that we may attain salvation and eternal life. So, those who are afraid to sacrifice themselves or to part with whatever they have in order to achieve their goals are successful failures! Sometimes we may sacrifice ourselves in prayers and fasting or by leaving our comfort zones for a while. In the Bible, we are told of king David who sacrificed himself for the great zeal he had for God's work.

"Surely I will not go into the chamber of my house, or go up to the comfort of my bed; I will not give sleep to my eyes or slumber to my eyelids, until I find a place for the Lord, a dwelling place for the Mighty One of Jacob." (Psalm 132:3-5) KJV

Only those who are ready to pay a price may succeed in life. And the more sacrifice we pay, the more successful we become.

6. TIME MANAGEMENT:
Time management is very important and it means a lot to our achievements. Those who have invested in time know how to manage it and it works for their successes. In a day, we have twenty-four hours. How then we utilize them will determine our successes or failures. Those who say they don't have time for doing certain things are just poor time managers. For good time managers know how to budget their time.

Out of the twenty-four hours in a day, serious people could budget them for God, work, leisure and sleep. It is very unfortunate that some people waste a lot of time doing things they are not meant to and may not even add some values in the lives, and they spend just little time in doing what could add some values in their lives and could as well help them to become successful in life.

There are many people including myself who testify how they have wasted many precious years doing useless or non-profiting things and how they have not been successful in life. If we want to become successful, then we shouldn't allow what we cannot do to interfere with what we can do. For the time we waste in doing what we cannot manage, is the time we should utilize in doing what we can manage. And besides, time wasted shall never be regained! We should learn to do our parts and what we cannot manage we should leave it to God.

7. DISCIPLINE IN WORD:
The words we speak matter a lot, for they can either hinder our successes or can work for our successes. This is so because there is power in confession. So then, whatever we confess that we become. So when we want to become successful we should avoid negative or discouraging words. Proverbs 18:21 states, ***"Death and life are in the power of the tongue and those who love it will eat its fruit."***

So, any negative or discouraging word we speak has the power to delay or stop our successes, and any positive word we speak has the power to make us become successful. So the choice is ours. In mathematics, when we add any greater negative integer to a smaller positive integer, the result we get is negative. For example - $8 + 4 = -4$.

And when we add negative to positive integers of the same number, the result is zero! For example $-12 + 12 = 0$. Here we can see that negatives are more powerful than positives and they are very influential in determining the results. We should therefore avoid negatives if our results are to be positive. For negativity eliminates positivity.

8. DISCIPLINE IN APPETITE:
Discipline in appetite would help especially beginners to become successful in their businesses. For high appetite causes us to become extravagant, and extravagance brings loses or failures to our businesses especially at the initial stage for it eats into savings and capital.

If we want to become successful in our businesses, we should wait until they begin to boom then we may start spending but still wisely.

9. SERIOUSNESS:
What crowns all other eight things mentioned above is seriousness. Without seriousness we may still not succeed in our endeavors. Though all other favorable factors to our successes may remain constant, even in the absence of seriousness, we may still not achieve our goals.

There are some people who have enough time, money, facilities or access to everything that could enable them succeed in all their pursuits; but because they lack seriousness, they end up achieving nothing!

Seriousness is therefore one of the most outstanding credentials in every successful person. Now when we decide to do something, we should do it seriously while observing everything that it takes for us to succeed. Those who reap the fruits of their prayers for instance, do not just pray as ordinary people but they seriously or diligently pray. And when this caliber of people decides to do something, they put their future in it with much diligence. Where going extra mile is needed to help us register success, only serious people may afford. And people who pass examinations with flying colors are the serious ones.

The following could then be the distinctive qualities in every serious person:
- A serious person is zealous.
- Learns from his past mistakes and avoids repeating them.
- Is not lazy but rather hardworking. He or she works tirelessly to accomplish his or her task.
- Has a teachable spirit.
- Maximizes his or her potential.
- Maximizes every opportunity or chance that presents itself on his or her way.
- Aims at excellent results.
- Does not easily give up until he or she sees tangible results.
- Is inquisitive and acquires new skills or ideas and puts them into use.

- ❖ Is a pragmatist, that is, he or she does things in a practical way rather than according to general theories
- ❖ Does not take things for granted.
- ❖ Is ever focused.
- ❖ Knows how to decide what his or her priorities are.
- ❖ Is a good time manager.
- ❖ Takes prompt actions while handling matters of urgency.

Seriousness is therefore very necessary if we should become successful in life and the secret of every successful person is hidden in seriousness!

CHAPTER NINE
DECISION FOR A COMEBACK

A person who needs a comeback or a return is the one who has either reached the point of no return, or has been dislodged from his or her original position; in either a forceful or deliberate manner. What takes people from their positions always comes with full force or power. Therefore, if we are to return to our original positions after being forced out, we should take a very bold decision in either a forceful or humble way depending on how we lost them.

The Bible narrates the story of the prodigal son especially how he left his position, and how again he returned to it after reaching the point of no return.

Then He said: "A certain man had two sons. And the younger of them said to his father, father, give me the portion of good that falls to me. So he divided to them his livelihood. And not many days after, the younger son gathered all together, journeyed to a far country, and there wasted his possessions with prodigal living. But when he had spent all, there arose a severe famine in that land and he began to be in want. Then he went and joined himself to a citizen of the country, and he sent him into his fields to feed swine. And he would gladly have filled his stomach with the pods that the swine ate, and no one gave him anything. But when he came to himself, he said, how many of my father's hired servants have bread enough and to spare, and I perish with hunger!

I will arise and go to my father, and will say to him, father, I have sinned against heaven and before you. And I am no longer worthy to be called your son. Make me like one of your hired servants. And he arose and came to his father. But when he was still a great way off, his father saw him and had compassion, and ran and fell on his neck and kissed him." (Luke 15:11 – 20) KJV.

In the verses mentioned above, we can notice that the prodigal son's decision to leave his original position was deliberate; and when things became tough, he had to humble himself to come back to his father's house. It was not logical for him to return with force since he had left his father's house deliberately with even the portion of goods that fell to him!

Being out of position may not necessarily mean leaving our positions and going elsewhere. At times, we may remain in the same position but when in the actual sense we are not operating to our best. The reasons for people not being in their original or rightful positions are different. To some it is because of their mistakes or sins. Others, it is because of other people's propaganda and in majority of cases it's because of Satan's revenging mind.

The fall of Adam and Eve made them lose their position of glory and this also affected the rest of mankind after them. God with His tender heart decided to send His Son Jesus Christ so that we may be restored to our position of glory! Romans 3:23 clearly states, **"For all have sinned and fall short of the glory of God"**. So Jesus Christ had to come to redeem us from this fallen state; reconcile us to God and restore us to the original position of glory! Whenever we therefore sin or dwell in sin, we lose our position of glory. In the Bible, we are told how King David pleaded with God to restore him after he had sinned.

"Create in me a clean heart, O God, and renew a steadfast spirit within me. Do not cast me away from Your presence, and do not take Your Holy Spirit from me. Restore to me the joy of Your Salvation, and uphold me by Your generous Spirit."(Psalm 51:10-12)KJV

In the verses above, it appears like David knew the secret of being in the position where he could behold God's glory, but sin had taken him away from this position. For when we sin or remain in the backslidden state, we get out of the position of glory and anything we do in sin; God's glory is not manifested. Now the choice is ours. We may decide to remain in sin and we stay away from the position of beholding God's glory, or we may decide to show remorse for our sins and then repent with true repentance, and we get back to the position of beholding God's glory!

There are many things and people who have lost their former glories and it would only take serious decisions to return to those former glories. For the lost glories to return, we should identify the things which could have caused their departure and we fix them right. The Bible says, **"The glory of this latter temple shall be greater than the former; says the Lord of hosts. And in this place I will give peace; says the Lord of host." (Haggai 2:9) NKJV**

In the verse given above, the Bible promises greatness of glory in the latter day's temple as compared to the former temple. But given the current backslidden state of the Churches, even the former glory may not manifest as it should be! So before we dream about the latter glory, we should first recover the former and at this point, ground that will usher us to the latter glory shall be leveled.

If we should retain our glories or the glory of anything, then we have to continuously observe the things that attract glory and guard against the things that repel glory.

Sometimes we lose our positions because of other people's propaganda. This normally happens when **'nasty-minded'** people for example, put defamatory accusations on us which may culminate in the loss of our positions; if no through investigations are carried out. It is vital to know that struggling for positions has nowadays become the order of the day. Because of this, some people have even gone to the extent of claiming the lives of others in order to maintain their positions!!!It's therefore advisable to allow God be our job security so He may fight for us when threatened or accused falsely.

The Bible tells us how Joseph lost his position while in the house of Potiphar, because of the wife of Potiphar's propaganda, and was later imprisoned. Joseph trusted in God and from prison, he was enthroned to the position of a "Prime Minister."

"Then Pharaoh said to Joseph, in as much as God has shown you all this, there is no one as discerning and wise as you. You shall be over my house and all my people shall be ruled according to your word; only in regard to the throne will I be greater than you. And Pharaoh said to Joseph, see, I have set you over all the land of Egypt. Then Pharaoh took his signet ring off his hand and put it on Joseph's hand; and he clothed him in garments of fine linen and put a gold chain around his neck. And he had him ride in the second chariot which he had; and they cried out before him, bow the knee! So he set him over all the land of Egypt. Pharaoh also said to Joseph, I am Pharaoh, and without your consent no man may lift his hand or foot in all the land of Egypt." (Genesis 41:39-44) NKJV.

For those who could be suffering a similar fate like that of Joseph, I counsel them not to fight back but just to trust in God. One day, God may not only restore you but He may also promote you to the highest position; even before the very eyes of your enemies, and they will have to subject to you!

Some people are not only out of their positions, but they have also not reached their positions of authority. This is more of spiritual than physical, for Satan is the man behind it. There is a place in the spiritual realm where everyone who has reached operates to the maximum. But Satan being fully aware of this truth hinders many from reaching it. Satan knows very well the importance of maintaining and being in a rightful position, for he was once in heaven before he was forced down here on the earth.

Indeed, Lucifer was in the position of a worship leader in heaven before he conceived in his heart the idea of seeking to be worshipped, and later he was fought and overpowered and forced out of heaven together with his angels. The book of Jude verse six states, **"And the angels who did not keep their proper domain, but left their own abode, He has reserved in everlasting chains under darkness for the judgement of the great day."**

After losing his position in heaven, Lucifer and his angels have now resorted to hindering God's children from being in their positions of authority. Their revenging attacks on God's children are clear signs of wrath and they do it jealously. So now, rather than just deciding to return to our lost positions, we should aim higher at reaching our positions of authority. There are many people who are restrained in many ways not because they have sinned, but because they are not operating from their positions of authority in the spiritual realm!

Just as we have ranks in the physical armed forces, so it is in the spiritual realm. Now any child of God who is highly ranked in the spiritual realm should not behave like any other ordinary or lowly ranked believer. If for instance someone is a general in the spiritual realm, Satan will assign wicked spiritual generals to attack him. So then, when this child of God underestimates his enemies, he will always suffer defeats in most of his battles. How then could one know his or her position in the spiritual realm?

The answer is simple, as we continue to engage Satan on fierce battles and we win, we also get promoted to another rank in the spiritual realm, and it is very easy for us to know whether or not we are serious fighters. Another thing which could also help us know our spiritual ranks is the calling upon our lives. For the bigger the calling or assignments here on the earth, the higher we are in ranks. That is why it is very vital for each and every child of God to prayerfully ask God and discover what on earth he or she was created for.

Just as God knows all of us, so is Satan. Satan knows us even with our ranks in the spiritual realm. So when he is fighting us individually, he knows how to handle us very well according to our ranks. If there is anything we should fight for very seriously, then it is our spiritual positions of authority. Satan knows very well that when we are in our rightful spiritual positions of authority, he wouldn't manage us and that is why he tries harder to keep many ignorant of this truth.

A moment we realize that we are out of our positions; we should then take serious decisions for a comeback. Those who feel they are already in the point of no return; I discourage them from hanging there for there is still hope for them. The first thing we should do is to come to our senses whenever we are out of our positions, and this requires us to always be in full possession of our mental faculties. For those who are in full possession of their mental faculties, have the power to reason radically and radical reasoning brings radical decision!

CHAPTER TEN
CHOOSING ON WHERE TO SPEND ETERNITY

The decisions we take now when we are still alive on this planet earth, will determine where we shall spend our eternal lives after departing this life. And where we have chosen to belong to while on this earth matters a lot as far as eternal inheritance is concerned. Those who have chosen to belong to the kingdom of Satan are the ones preparing for eternal death. And those who have chosen to belong to the kingdom of God are the ones preparing for eternal life. It's vital to know that there is no middle ground in belonging to any of the two kingdoms mentioned above. For it's either we belong to God's kingdom or we belong to Satan's kingdom.

What qualifies us to belong to any of the two kingdoms mentioned above is the fulfillment of their requirements. For these two kingdoms have different requirements. So, the basis of the foundations of the throne for these two conflicting kingdoms is where we can derive the requirements from.

For God's kingdom, the Bible says, **"Righteousness and justice are the foundation of Your throne; mercy and truth go before Your face." (Psalm 89:14) KJV**

Anyone who therefore diligently practices righteousness and justice with mercy and truth as part and parcel of him or her qualifies to belong to this kingdom. For Satan's kingdom, the reverse is true. For his is based on unrighteousness and injustice and his "war-like countenance" is full of mercilessness and deceit! Whoever therefore practices unrighteousness and injustice with a merciless and a heart full of deceit, qualifies to be in this kingdom.

The preparations and decisions for where one wants to spend his or her eternity should be made now when the being is still there. For after death, one begins his or her "hereafter life". One thing is true, none wants to spend their eternity in hell, but because of ignorance, some people will perish in hell; for their unfruitful works that promote the kingdom of darkness will guarantee a place for them in hell! Now spending eternity in heaven is not for every Tom, Dick and Harry; but for those who have taken serious decisions to completely abandon the unfruitful works of darkness, and they begin to become heaven minded.

It's important to know that Jesus Christ is not coming back for every Church, but for the one having no spot or wrinkle; or a holy one without any blemish. So for those who would like to spend their eternity in heaven, the set standard for qualification is holiness and righteousness. Our decisions for spending eternity in heaven should then meet the standard for qualification. There is no way we can bribe God in order to enter into heaven without the required qualifications. For the Bible says, "**Nevertheless, the solid foundation of God stands, having this seal: "The Lord knows those who are His," and let everyone who names the name of Christ depart from iniquity." (2 Timothy 2:19) KJV.**

Much as God wants everyone to go to heaven, but He is also not ignorant to the fact that some will refuse Him and choose to go to hell. And that explains why Jesus Christ said in the book of Matthew 22:14, **"For many are called but few are chosen."** It is then essential to note that God's selection of the inheritors of His kingdom is solely on merit. It's either we deserve or we do not!

In the same book of Matthew 7:21 – 23, Jesus said; "**Not everyone who says to Me, Lord, Lord, shall enter the Kingdom of heaven, but he who does the will of My Father in heaven. Many will say to Me in that day, Lord, Lord, have we not prophesized in Your name, cast out demons in Your name, and done many wonders in Your name ? And then I will declare to them, I never knew you; depart from Me, you who practice lawlessness!"**

Many people including some servants of God are under the illusion that, by the virtue of naming the name of Christ or serving God; they qualify to enter God's Kingdom. This is not the case according to Jesus Christ. For one may decide to serve God while dwelling in sin and he miss's heaven still! Serving God is therefore one thing and working out our Christianity or showing true Christian qualities is also another thing.

Now the choice is ours. For we may decide to name the name of Christ or serve God and at the same time behave in a very unchristian way or simply practice lawlessness and we end up in hell; or we may decide to behave in a very Christian way while also serving God and we make it to heaven!

Inheriting God's Kingdom is therefore not as easy as many might suppose, for Satan is also on high competition for souls. In fact the greatest mission of Satan is to win as many souls as he can to hell, for this is his consolation given that there is no hope for him to inherit God's Kingdom. Jesus Christ made some challenging remarks concerning entering into heaven and going to hell, for He said:

"Enter by the narrow gate; for wide is the gate and broad is the way that leads to destruction, and there are many who go in by it. Because narrow is the gate and difficult is the way which leads to life, and there are few who find it." (Matthew 7:13 -14) NKJV

The verses above should then provoke us to seriousness, for Jesus Christ gave a very "clear–cut difference" between the gates which lead people to destruction and life.   Satan has made it very easy for his disciples to enter the gate which leads to destruction. For there is no resistance for those who enter into hell, they just have to qualify and then wait for their "voyages" to this place of condemnation. It really grieves God that some have chosen to go to hell and yet He has prepared many mansions in heaven for His children! **"Do I have any pleasure at all that the wicked should die? Says the Lord, and not that he should turn from his ways and live?"(Ezekiel 18:23) NKJV**

Let's always be reminded that Satan is working around the clock to accomplish his mission of leading many to hell, for he knows very well that even Jesus' second coming is around the corner. Some of us could be relaxed about this truth, but as for Satan, he is well informed and is actively working on "trial and error method."

Jesus Christ in the book of Matthew 11:12 said, **"And from the time of John the Baptist until now the Kingdom of God suffers violence; and the violent take it by force." NKJV**

This statement made by Jesus Christ, is yet to remind us of what manner of seriousness we should exhibit in making decisions that will show us as inheritors of God's Kingdom. For where there is violence, there is resistance, and to overcome resistance; we should apply force. Now the resistance we face in entering into heaven is from Satan for it is his yearning desire to hinder many from going to heaven.

Entering into heaven has never been an easy thing. It's all about war, and which war is not physical but rather spiritual. As points of ponder, one could ask himself or herself these questions: where do I intend to spend my eternity; in heaven or in hell? If in heaven, do I qualify to enter into it like even tomorrow in case I happen to depart this life? According to my Christian qualities, where do I belong to presently; To God's kingdom or Satan's kingdom? What strategies have I worked out to overcome the things that hinder people from entering into heaven? If Jesus comes tomorrow, will He find me prepared or unprepared? May the questions above guide us to make meaningful decisions and preparations that will book a place for us in heaven!

Since it is certain that entering into heaven is not a joke, we should then prepare for it vigorously!! For when we fail to prepare for anything, then we prepare to fail. So those who fail to prepare for heaven, they prepare to fail to enter into it and instead make it to hell. But choosing to go to hell is nothing other than doing oneself a **"grave injustice."** For in hell, there is crying and gnashing of teeth in agonizing manner!

The following counsels could help us in our preparations for going to heaven: *Let's accept Jesus Christ as our Lord and Savior, work out our salvation with fear and trembling while diligently observing the do's and don'ts of God's word, obey God by doing His will; with unceasing prayers we should defend our positions as God's children while also protecting our faith, and in the strongest possible terms, we should refuse to compromise God's righteousness and holiness.*

We should also refuse to surrender to the will of Satan. Let's therefore choose heaven and avoid hell for hell is not a place to be. And we should also begin to behave like the inhabitants of heaven who are ever in worshipping God. And this way, we shall by all means make it to heaven.

CHAPTER ELEVEN
DECIDING ON HOW TO ACQUIRE WEALTH

The decisions we make to acquire material things or money are worthwhile considering, for there are those who get theirs in an honest way and those who obtain theirs in a devious or dishonest way. Those who obtain theirs in an honest way, they either prayerfully labor for them or miraculously get them from God after requesting for them in prayer.

Those who get theirs in a dishonest way, they get by plundering, stealing or robbing and sometimes even claiming the lives of the rightful owners, under false pretense, by misappropriation, embezzlement or corruption; by accepting a bribe, and seeking those who are mediums to consult for them spirits, demons or Satan to give them riches. There are those who have gone to the extent of sacrificing human beings and worst of all their own children, just to appease gods so that they may become wealthy!

Today, there are many people who are very rich but the source of their riches are questionable for they neither labor nor make their requests known to God in prayer. The Bible says, **"Wealth gained by dishonesty will be diminished, but he who gathers by labor will increase." (Proverbs 13:11).** So those who have gained wealth dishonestly, their wealth will not only be diminished, but it will also affect the generations after them! There are some people who are poverty-stricken because of the curses they inherited from their forefathers.

The Bible says, **"A good man leaves an inheritance to his children's children, but the wealth of the sinner is stored up for the righteous." (Proverbs 13:22)**

It is really very sad to note that some people will gather wealth for others whereas their own descendants will remain wanting! This is so because God punishes iniquity up to the third or fourth generation.

" For I; the Lord your God am Jealous God; visiting the iniquity of the forefathers upon the children to the third and fourth generation of those who hate Me, but showing mercy to thousands, to those who love Me and keep My commandments." (Exodus 20: 5b -6) NKJV.

May the verses above serve as a reminder, for they clearly bring God's stand on those who gain wealth dishonestly. Indeed, there are many people who did terrible bad things in the past and their descendants are now reaping horribly! There are those who murdered to take others' possessions, others sacrificed human beings to obtain wealth; some accepted bribes and others practiced witchcraft to gather riches. Though they are long–gone, but the "long–drawn–out" breakthroughs of their descendants are attributable to them.

The Bible says, **"The blessing of the Lord makes one rich; and He adds no sorrow with it." (Proverbs 10:22) KJV.** So rather than remaining sorrowful because of the riches we have gained dishonestly, we should then allow God to bless us and we remain peaceful even leaving an inheritance to our children and children's children.

For those who have chosen to get blessings from God, they should entirely depend on Him while also carefully observing His instructions. The Bible tells us God's plans or thoughts towards us as His children, for it say;

"For I know the thoughts that I think toward you, says the Lord, thoughts of peace and not of evil, to give you a future and a hope." (Jeremiah 29:11) NKJV

We should then avoid making copies to acquire wealth for God's plans towards every child of His are different and unique. God knows what one should do in order to get blessings or acquire wealth. So it is upon us to ask Him of those good plans He has towards us so that we may become partakers of His blessings.

Some people these days give false testimonies on how they acquired their wealth. They even use the name of God whenever they testify. For in this manner they speak, "Oh, I really thank God for He has given me a car, house, money or any material thing," but when the truth is; they obtained them dishonestly! Let's learn to allow God Himself bless us so that we may give clean testimonies to encourage others.

We should really feel ashamed whenever we testify falsely. And it's important to realize that "Ill-gotten wealth is like cancer of the bone." We may testify falsely, but those very things we have acquired dishonestly will soon begin to "eat us up" like cancer eating up the bone!

Many people do hinder God from intervening in their affairs, for they may pray to God all right, but they may not be patient enough to wait for their answers. To date, God still intervenes supernaturally, but where there is dishonesty - He keeps Himself a loof. When we want to see God's supernatural intervention, we should then avoid dishonesty and doing things ordinarily.

As points of ponder, one may ask himself these questions: Where is the source of my wealth? Is it from God or Satan? Whom do I honor with my riches; God or Satan? The very vehicle I drive, the house I dwell in, the many plots I have acquired, the fat account I have and the money I use to cater for the welfare of my house, how did I obtain them? Am I honest or dishonest? Is God pleased with the way I acquire my wealth? How did my forefathers acquire their riches? Honestly or dishonestly? If dishonestly, would I love to allow history repeat itself?

May the previous questions help us to make wise decisions to acquire wealth so that even when our riches are increasing, we shall remain at peace and we shall be channels of blessings to the poor and needy. If one's source of wealth is from God, they should consider blessing others too. So the blessings or riches we have must affect others if they are really from God.

Dear child of God, after reading this chapter of the book and you discover that there are some touching things that would need some prayers, in this manner you could then pray:

Heavenly Father in Jesus' name, I would like to say thank You for revealing this truth to me. For I now know which decisions I should make to acquire riches that would leave no sorrow in my life. Lord God, I repent on my behalf and on behalf of my forefathers for the things we acquired by dishonesty (mention those things to God). Forgive me and my forefathers oh Lord, for we have sinned and acted wickedly before You. Dear Lord, I pray that let this be a turning point in my life and this day forth, help me to order my conduct aright so that I may acquire riches by honesty. Lord God, it's written in the book of proverbs 22:4 that **"By humility and the fear of the Lord are riches and honor and life".** *I pray then that You may cloth me with humility and fill me with the Spirit of fear of You so that I may obtain riches, honor and life as Your word stipulates. Merciful Father, You have promised in Your Holy Bible to bless the work of one's hands. Now basing on this promise oh Lord, I pray that You may bless the work of my hands and shower me with multiple blessings for I would like to be a channel of blessing to many. Thank You Lord for all the way You have intervened in my affairs, in Jesus' most powerful and wonder working name I have prayed and believed. Amen.*

CHAPTER TWELVE
CHOOSING ON WHOM OR WHAT TO SERVE

Serving somebody or something is a choice. We may therefore choose to serve whoever or whatever. We may serve in four different ways that is, serving God, man, Satan and mammon. But in this chapter of the book, I will mainly debate on serving God and Satan. Indeed, there is none who does not serve either of the two. Some people double it by serving both of them! But deciding to serve God Is the best of all other decisions we make in life, and out of it; a big reward awaits whoever finishes well. God expects every child of His to be serving Him alone, for He is the Father and creator of all mankind.

Though we may serve God in various ways, but there are some people who still do not consider serving Him, for they have wrong perceptions about it. They think it's only for some specific people. But in the book of Colossians 2:23, it's written, **"And whatever you do, do it heartily, as to the Lord and not men."** So whatever we do heartily even if it's someone else's work, God regards it as ministry and those who do their works this way are God's true ministers!

Medical personnel are God's ministers to the sick and wounded, they only ought to do their medical services heartily as though to God.

Teachers are also God's ministers to learners, only what is expected from them is professionalism in their teachings. All other civil servants are God's ministers too, only they have to perform well in their civil services with no cases of corruption or bribery on them.

Business people are God's ministers as well. They just have to serve their clients honestly. Those who use weighing scales in their businesses should avoid dishonest ones, for they are an abomination to God. Casual laborers, slaves or hired servants are yet God's ministers, but they have to be faithful and obedient to their masters. Similarly, masters are also God's servants. They then have to give their bondservants what is just and fair not forgetting that they also have a master in heaven. Armed forces are God's ministers as well, only they should be contented with their pay not even intimidating the citizens. Clergymen or pastors are God's ministers, only what is required of them is doing God's will and work, without deceit – even avoiding practicing moral laxity.

So, any work we do deceitfully, or not in the same manner as given above; whether it's someone else's work or one's own, this kind is detestable in God's sight. And whatever God hates – is Satan's number one choice. So then, knowingly or unknowingly, but whoever is involved in this kind of practice; this one is no longer a true minister of God and he or she qualifies to become a minister of Satan!

The circumstances under which we may serve God are in three different ways: There are those who decide to serve God willingly on their own. Other people become God's ministers after being called by other ministers of God or on people's request. And there are those whom God Himself calls into ministry. All these three categories of people are God's servants and God regards all of them as His ministers. The only difference is in the dispensation of the grace of God. For those who are called by God into ministry, they have greater dispensation of the grace. What other ministers of God may not bear or handle, this category has that special grace to tackle it!

In the Bible, we are told the circumstance under which Paul came into ministry for it is written, **"Paul; an apostle not from men nor through man, but through Jesus Christ and God the Father who raised Him from the dead." (Galatians 1:1) KJV**

The verse mentioned clearly tells us that Paul's ministry was as a result of God calling him, and the dispensation of God's grace upon him was incomparable to the rest of the then ministers! So when we choose to serve God, we should consider how we are going to begin lest we start envying other ministers' grace.

It's vital for us to know that God's redemptive purposes for nations, families, organizations or individuals are different and yet they are for ministry. So it's upon us to discover from God His redemptive purposes for our nations, families, organizations or individual lives. It is of great significance to serve God in the very area He redeemed us for. For right there - there is grace, protection and provision! So as many as are those who walk aimlessly, these are the ones who have not yet discovered God's redemptive purposes on their lives. In other words, these are the people who do not know what God created them for or the reasons for their living on this planet earth.

Now regardless of the circumstances under which we may become God's ministers, but whoever desires to serve God must first sit down and count the cost and see what is required of him. In the Bible, we are given some of the qualifications we should meet in order to serve God.

"This is a faithful saying: If a man desires the position of a bishop, he desires a good work. A bishop then must be blameless, the husband of one wife, temperate, sober-minded, of good behavior, hospitable, able to teach; not given to wine, not violent, not greedy for money, but gentle, not quarrelsome, not covetous; one who rules his own house well, having his children in submission with all reverence. For if a man does not know how to rule his own house, how will he take care of the Church of God?" (1 Timothy 3:1-5) KJV

The qualifications in the previous verses above do not only apply to bishops, but also to every servant of God. Now ministry begins from a family and anyone who cannot manage the affairs of his house, cannot manage God's house as well. So then, the decisions we make to serve God must also help us to meet the qualifications of serving Him.

Much as God wants us to serve Him alone, but Satan also rivals for the same. Indeed, Satan is ever fighting "tooth and nail" to see to it that he wins as many ministers as he can to serve him. Because of this struggle, he has even managed to cause some people to serve two masters, that is, God and him! But the Bible gives the danger of serving two masters, for it says: **"No one can serve two masters; for either he will hate the one and love the other, or he will be loyal to the one and despise the other. You cannot serve God and mammon." (Matthew 6:24) KJV**

In the verse above, it's very clear that serving two masters are impossible. It's really sad to note that Satan has made some ministers of God to become "double-dealers" for they say one thing and mean another.

In other words, they do not practice what they preach! But as for me, I would encourage everybody to serve only one master, who is none other than God the creator of visible and invisible things.

The truth is, Satan is not pleased with whoever has decided to serve God for he knows that this one is no longer his. So the best he can afford is to fight, intimidate or terrify this person. In fact, Satan does not wait for any invitation to come and fight us - as long as we have decided to serve God. This is not to discourage us but rather to create awareness so that we may begin ministry when we are well equipped and well enough to.

The Bible says, **"And not in any way terrified by your adversaries, which is to them a proof of perdition, but to you of salvation, and that from God." (Philippians 1:28) KJV**

Satan will never give up in terrifying us for this is how he can detect those who are really determined in serving God, and those who may defect to his camp so that they may serve him. That explains why whenever God is commissioning someone to ministry He urges them to be of good courage, for He is aware of hard times in ministry. In the Bible, we are told how He commissioned Joshua to replace Moses in the ministry.

For He said to him, **"Be strong and of good courage, for to this people you shall divide as an inheritance the land which I swore to their fathers to give them. Only be strong and very courageous, that you may observe to do according to all the law which Moses My servant commanded you; do not turn from it to the right hand or to the left, that you may prosper wherever you go."** *(Joshua 1:6 – 7) NKJV*

Whoever has made up their mind to serve God should then learn to encourage themselves, less they begin to waver their determination especially when faced with raging or challenging storms. The phrase "fear not," appears many times in the Bible, for fear is the greatest weapon of Satan to discourage God's ministers. For once we fear anything then we shall by all means fail to handle it!

Satan knows this truth very well, and that is why he also instills boldness in his ministers to fight God's ministers. Imagine the level of boldness in those who sacrifice their own children, those who murder, those who exhume dead and sometimes even stinking bodies at night and those who eat human flesh!! Aren't these Satan's ministers? In fact, those who have filled this earth with great terror are Satan's ministers. Whose ministers are the terrorists, suicide bombers and robbers? They are certainly Satan's.

Here I am not trying to exalt Satan's ministers, but rather urging God's ministers to wake up. For when really shall this portion of scripture that says, **"Who is he who overcomes the world, but he who believes that Jesus is the Son of God?"** Be fulfilled in some ministers of God? It is really sad to note that some of those whom the scripture above would be fulfilled on, are instead victims of the circumstance. For instead of overcoming the world, it's the other way round!

In the Bible, we are told of some ministers of God whose manner of determination in serving Him is remarkable. Joshua for one was a very determined servant of God. For he said to the Israelites; **"Now therefore, fear the Lord, serve Him in sincerity and truth, and put away the gods which your fathers served on the other side of the River and in Egypt. Serve the Lord! And if it seems evil to you to serve the Lord, choose for yourselves this day whom you will serve, whether gods which your fathers served that were on the other side of the River, or of the gods of the Amorites, in whose land you dwell. But as for me and my house, we will serve the Lord." (Joshua 24:14-15) NKJV**

In the verses above, we can clearly see that Joshua's decision of serving God did not depend on anybody. For he was determined to serve God together with his house even when the rest of the Israelites were not ready to!

Sadrach, Meshach and Abed–Nego were also other determined ministers of God who defied king Nebuchadnezzar's decree of worshipping the gold image and serving his gods. For it's written, **"Nebuchadnezzar spoke, saying to them, " is it true, Sadrach, Meshach, and Abed – Nego, that you do not serve my gods and worship the gold image which I have set up? Now if you are ready at the time you hear the sound of the horn, flute, harp, lyre, and psaltery, in symphony with all kinds of music, and you fall down and worship the image which I have made, good! But if you do not worship, you shall be cast immediately into the midst of a burning fiery furnace. And who is the god who will deliver you from my hands?" Sadrach, Meshach and Abed –Nego answered and said to the king, "O Nebuchadnezzar, we have no need to answer you in this matter. If that is the case, our God whom we serve is able to deliver us from your hands, O king. But if not, let it be known to you, king, that we do not serve your gods, nor will we worship the gold image which you have set up." (Daniel 3:14-18) NKJV**

Under normal circumstance, the three men mentioned above would have feared king Nebuchadnezzar and a burning fiery furnace. But because they had madly fallen in love with God, even saturated with an "air of fierce determination;" they chose to be thrown into the burning fiery furnace! Apostle Paul in the Bible was a man with a nature just like any servant of God of this generation. But his unwavering boldness and determination in serving God is worthwhile emulating.

This was the minister of God who declared that nothing could separate him from loving and serving Him! For he said, "**For I am persuaded that neither death nor life, nor angels nor principalities nor powers, nor things present nor things to come. Nor height nor depth, nor any other created thing shall be able to separate us from the love of God which is in Christ Jesus our Lord". (Romans 8:38-39)KJV.** The verses above clearly show Paul's manner of determination in serving God, and no wonder when spoke these words; "**Then Paul answered, what do you mean by weeping and breaking my heart? For I am ready not only to be bound, but also to die at Jerusalem for the name of the Lord Jesus". (Acts 21:13)KJV**

Death is what is most feared by almost everyone on this planet earth. But for Paul who spoke of his readiness even to die, he must have then been a very brave and determined servant of God!

May we then learn from the men of God mentioned above so that when it comes to serving God, we may take fierce decisions, and when it comes to refusing to serve Satan; we may uncompromisingly denounce him for he is not our creator. There are three things we have to consider if we should effectively serve God:

Preparations:
Much as we may decide to serve God, but it takes preparations for us to become successful. And how prepared or unprepared we are, will determine our successes and failures in our ministries. We may prepare as a nation, family, an organization or individually – but according to God's calling or redemptive purposes upon us. There are many people, nations, organizations and families with bigger callings–but unpreparedness has delayed their ministries!

Those whom God has called as "international figures" for instance, should prepare themselves to meet international standard. So, anything below this will eminently hinder them. For they have to behave like internationals, reason like them, they should also carry the burdens of nations of the world in their hearts - even paying the price by praying or interceding for them; or just doing anything that is expected from any other international person. For the bigger the calling, the bigger the challenges we may encounter .Another way we may also prepare ourselves is by overcoming our weaknesses and the things which could be hindering us from serving God.

One thing we should get rid of is the reproach. A reproach is anything that brings shame upon us. It could be sin, poverty, misfortune, late marriage, incurable disease, being childless, being in a state of indebtedness, being sexually abused by demons, and being homeless just to mention but a few. Reproaches are terribly bad things – even God is very concerned about our reproachful lives.

In the Bible, we are told how God dealt with the reproach of His children the Israelites. For it is written, **"Then the Lord said to Joshua, this day I have rolled away the reproach of Egypt from you. Therefore the name of the place is called Gilgal to this day." (Joshua 5:9) NKJV**

God had to roll away the reproach of His children for He knew it would hinder them from serving Him. Much as God is the only One who can roll away our reproaches, it's still upon us to request Him to roll them away from us. Now Satan being exceedingly jealous with God's ministers puts reproaches on them so that they may fail to serve God. The truth is, as long as we still have reproaches on us, life will never be pleasant and we shall as well be limited in serving God!

The ministry according to Jesus Christ:
If we should serve God perfectly, then we have to emulate Jesus' ministry. And the secret of Jesus' ministry was in the seven Spirits He was filled with. Those seven Spirits were prophesied before His birth by prophet Isaiah. For it is written, ***"There shall come forth a Rod from the stem of Jesse, and a Branch shall grow out of His roots. The Spirit of the Lord shall rest upon Him, the Spirit of wisdom and understanding, the Spirit of counsel and might, the Spirit of knowledge and the fear of the Lord." (Isaiah 11:1-2) NKJV.***

The seventh Spirit that was also upon Jesus Christ but not mentioned here was that of Kingship or Lordship. This Spirit of kingship or Lordship manifested on Jesus Christ the day He triumphantly entered Jerusalem while sitting on a donkey. **(See the book of Matthew Chapter 21:1-11).**

Jesus Christ needed no counsel from others for He had the Spirit of counsel upon Him. The Spirit of wisdom helped Him to behave wisely, the Spirit of understanding made it possible for Him to understand things in depth, the Spirit of might empowered Him for ministry and the Spirit of fear of the Lord kept Him unspotted from the World!

Satan also apart from the Spirit of fear of the Lord fills his ministers with similar spirits as mentioned above, though his are for doing evil. So if this be the case with Satan's ministers, how then should God's ministers desire to be filled with them? There is a very great difference between God's ministers with and without the seven Spirits mentioned above. Any servant of God who has the Spirit of fear of the Lord for example, will always fear God – even keeping himself unspotted from shameful scandals. But the one without the same will always be spotted in shameful scandals.

Growth to maturity
Much as one may adamantly decide to serve God, but growth to maturity is required of him. For one's level of maturity determines how he can handle the ministry. Growth is a choice. We can choose to grow or not to grow. Now physical growth may not necessarily mean maturity. One could be well advanced in age yet his actions are always dominated by elements of immaturity. But spiritual growth is not measured by age. For one could be in his or her tender age yet spiritually mature!

In the Bible, we are given Paul's remarks about maturity and immaturity. For he said, **"When I was a child, I spoke as a child, I understood as a child, I thought as a child; but when I became a man I put away childish things." (I Corinthians 13:11) KJV**

In the verses given above, Apostle Paul gave an example about himself concerning immaturity and maturity. Remarks can be used as a yardstick to measure their immaturity and maturity for both spiritual and physical growth. According to Paul, immature person speaks, understands and thinks as a child whereas mature one like an adult.

Jesus Christ had twelve disciples and out of them, three namely Peter, James and John; were in the inner core and they were most loved by Him. As a case in point, Peter and Thomas were both disciples of Jesus Christ. But Peter was a mature minister whereas Thomas was immature one. In the Bible, we are given at least two different instances where Peter exercised maturity and also two different instances where Thomas showed immaturity.

One instance in which Peter showed maturity was when he confessed Jesus as the Christ. For its written, **"when Jesus came in the region of Caesarea Philippi, He asked His disciples, saying, who do men say that I, the Son of Man, am? So they said, some say John the Baptist, some Elijah, and others Jeremiah or one of the prophets. He said to them, "But who do you say I am?" Simon Peter answered and said, "You are the Christ, the Son of the living God," Jesus answered and said to him, "Blessed are you, Simon Bar–Jonah, for flesh and blood has not revealed this to you, but My Father who is in heaven." (Matthew 16:13-17) NKJV**

In the verses above, it's very clear that only Peter revealed exactly who Jesus Christ was and is even to date. Peter's maturity helped him to know the One he was following and serving.

Another instance where Peter exhibited maturity in was the day he walked on the water. For it's written, **"Now in the fourth watch of the night Jesus went to them walking on the sea, they were troubled, saying, it is a ghost! And they cried out for fear. But immediately Jesus spoke to them saying, "Be of good cheer! It is I; do not be afraid. And Peter answered Him and said, "Lord, if it's You, command me to come to You on the water." So He said, "come." And when Peter had come down out of the boat, he walked on the water to go to Jesus." (Matthew 14:25 – 29) NKJV**

In the verses above, it is very evident that Peter's level of faith was higher than the rest of the disciples. For it takes faith for someone to take an action similar to the one Peter took. Now, no wonder, for when it pleased Jesus Christ that Peter was mature enough; He commissioned him to spearhead the ministry after His ascension to heaven.

One instance in which Thomas showed immaturity was when he spoke childishly concerning Lazarus' death .For it's written, **"Then Jesus said to them plainly, Lazarus is dead. And I am glad for your sakes that I was not there that you may believe. Nevertheless let us go to him. Then Thomas, who is called Didymium, said to his fellow disciples, "Let us also go, that we may die with him." (John 11:14-16) KJV**

Only immature person would speak like Thomas concerning somebody's death. But a mature person would talk of mourning with or consoling the bereaved.

Another instance in which Thomas also showed immaturity was when he doubted Jesus' resurrection. For its written, **"Now Thomas, called the twin, one of the twelve, was not with them when Jesus came. The other disciples therefore said to him, "We have seen the Lord." So he said to them, "unless I see in His hands the print of the nails, and put my finger into the print of the nails, and put my hand into His side, I will not believe." (John 20:24 – 25) KJV.**

In the verses above, Thomas' immaturity is clearly seen. For unbelief is a sign of immaturity. Thomas did not believe in his fellow disciples – neither in Jesus Christ. For Jesus Christ had said before His death that "He would die and resurrect on the third day." To date, there are some ministers of God who are like Thomas. This is so because they have chosen not to grow to maturity!

If we may measure growth in terms of percentage; then there are those who would fall below average, others just on average, some above average and there are those who would really excel. It's then of great importance to know the level of our growth in all aspects of our lives. If for instance one wants to know the level of his growth in faith, he should then just consider the things he fears and the ones he doesn't fear. For fear is number one enemy of faith. So then, as many as are the things we fear, with the only exception of fearing God or to sin, this is a clear indication of having little faith – and the reverse is true.

Now taking 0- 49 percent as being below average, 50 percent as being on average, 51–74 percent as being above average and 75-100 percent as being the cut-off marks for excelling; then those who fall in the first group at least – fear up to 51 things and that obviously show them as those with very little faith, those who fall in the second group at least–fear 50 things and their faith is fifty percent.

Those who fall in the third group are the ones who fear relatively few things and they can easily grow in faith–even to the point of excelling. Those who fall in the fourth group are the people who are not easily moved, and in most cases, these are the ones who do great things!

There are around five areas which any servant of God ought to grow in, and these are faith, hope, love, patience and obedience. Now as long as we do not excel in the five areas mentioned above, we shall always find difficulties in serving God. So then, any servant of God who falls below average or just on average in the five areas mentioned above, this one's ministry will always be shaky and it will also delay to flourish.

This question might readily come especially on how to grow in the five areas mentioned above, and the question is, "how could one grow in faith, love, hope, patience and obedience?" To grow in any of the five areas mentioned above is upon everyone individually. Jesus Christ Himself had to learn obedience by the things which He suffered! For the book of Hebrews chapter five verse eight says, **"Though He was a Son, yet He learned obedience by the things which He suffered."**

In the Bible, we are given how Jesus Christ rebuked and challenged His disciples' faithlessness. For it's written, **"Then Jesus Christ answered and said, "O faithless and perverse generation, how long shall I be with you? How long shall I bear with you? Bring him here to Me". And Jesus rebuked the demon, and it came out from him; and the child was cured from that very hour. Then the disciples came to Jesus privately and said, "Why could we not cast it out? So Jesus said to them, "Because of your unbelief; for assuredly, I say to you, if you have faith as a mustard seed, you will say to this mountain, move from here to there and it will move; and nothing will be impossible for you." (Matthew 17:17-20) NKJV.**

Another instance where Jesus Christ talked to His disciples concerning faith was when He was teaching them on forgiveness. For it's written, **"Take heed to yourselves. If your brother sins against you, rebuke him; and if he repents, forgive him.**
And if he sins against you seven times in a day, and seven times in a day returns to you, saying, I repent, you shall forgive him. And the apostles said to the Lord, "increase our faith". So the Lord said, if you have faith as a mustard seed, you can say to this mulberry tree, "Be pulled up by the roots and be planted in the sea, and it would obey you." (Luke 17: 3-6) KJV.

In the verses above, the disciples thought by asking Jesus to increase their faith, He would probably pray for them or command faith to come upon them. But it did not happen that way, for Jesus Christ in His response to their request of increasing their faith said; "if you have faith as a mustard seed, you can say to this mulberry tree, be pulled up by the roots and be planted in the sea, and it would obey you".

Growing in faith is therefore upon everyone on individual basis. To date, some people still seek counselling and prayers so that they may love others, have patience and obedience, remain hopeful and for their faith to increase. But unlike in other areas where we can be prayed for, in the five areas mentioned above we just have to develop, nurture and cultivate them!

The Bible in the book of James chapter two verse seventeen says, **"Thus also faith by itself, if it does not have works, is dead."** So, if one wants to grow in faith – he shouldn't just pray to God to increase his faith but rather do the works of faith. For each time we take actions of faith, we also grow in faith–and thus increasing our faith as well.

As points of ponder, may the following questions guide us in making decision on whom to serve: whom do I serve, God or Satan? If God, is He pleased with my works or not? But if Satan, what does it really profit me to serve him? Is the decision I have made to serve God on a firm foundation or a weaker one? When weighed in the balances of God, shall I be found not wanting or wanting? How does God regard me, as a vessel of honor or as a vessel of dishonor? When faced with challenges, shall I still continue to serve God or I will give up?

I have asked the questions above with profound concern, with the hope that they will help us know whom to serve, to reaffirm our decisions of serving God; to reconsider the decision of serving two masters, and to prepare ourselves ready to face any challenge we may encounter in serving God and overcoming it.

A special prayer:
The following prayers could help those who have made up their minds to serve God. Even those who have not but have the desire to serve Him they could still work for them. You may pray after this manner: *Father in Jesus' name, I would like to appreciate You and say thank You for having made known to me the mysteries of serving You. For I now know the hidden things about serving You.*
I also now know whom or what to serve. And it's only You alone whom I should serve. Now dear Lord, I pray that You may allow Your Holy Spirit to continually guide me so that I may do things that are pleasing in Your sight; so that when weighed in Your balances I wouldn't be found wanting.

Heavenly Father, I have realized that it's of great significance to serve You in the area You redeemed me for. Now I pray, reveal to me the purpose of my living on this planet earth and / or what You redeemed me for so that I may begin to pursue it and hence serving You in that very area. Dear Lord, even as I have decided to serve You alone, I pray that You may cloth me with humility so that You may give me grace instead of resisting me.

I also pray that You may fill me with the Spirit of wisdom and understanding, counsel and might, knowledge and the fear of You. Dear Father, it's also my earnest prayer that You may mould and make me what You want me to be, so I may serve You as a vessel of honor and never as a vessel of dishonor. Oh Lord, I have also realized that preparations are of the essence as far as serving You is concerned. Now I pray to You Lord, help me in my areas of weaknesses and always allow Your Holy Spirit to remind me to be prepared for it will help me to serve You even in hard times. Dear Lord, as a sign of reaffirmation, this day forth I have pledged allegiance to You with all my strength and all I am – and with all the faculties within me.

Help me to always show a loyal and perfect heart to You, so that You may always prove Yourself strong on my behalf. Lord God, I also pray that You may roll away all my reproaches for these are hindrances in serving You and besides, I do not want Your name to be blasphemed among the heathen because of my reproachful life. I pray all these in Jesus' name. Amen.

CONCLUSION

In this book, I have tried the best I know how to give precise details about decision-making. It has always been my heart's desire and prayer to reach God's children with what "He" the Lord has put in my heart. Nevertheless, it had never been easy for me to figure out how and when to begin. But thanks to God, for when it pleased Him – He told me to begin writing books as one of the ways of reaching His people!

Indeed, It isn't easy to fathom God's ways and thoughts for it came to pass that this portion of scripture that says, **"For My thoughts are not your thoughts, nor are your ways My ways says the Lord. For as the heavens are higher than the earth, so are my ways higher than your ways, and My thoughts than your thoughts",** vividly came to fulfillment on me. As a matter of fact, before I started writing books–I could hardly see the gift of writing in me. But as for God, that was His thought towards me – as His minister, and His way I should follow as far as beginning ministry is concerned!

GLOSSARY

The words and expressions which are in the glossary are alphabetically arranged, so in case you would like to know the meaning of the word or expression you are not very sure about; just look for it in alphabetical order as given below.

Aa

Adamantly: Done in a more conservative way without showing readiness to change attitude or mind. Those who have adamantly decided to serve God are the ones who have made up their minds on a very serious note to serve Him.

Adhere: To stick or super glue to somebody.
An arm and a leg: To cost an arm and a leg is to reap unpleasantly after making a wrong decision.

Bb

Befitting: That which is appropriate.

Cc

Calculated risk: Doing something with the full knowledge of what might happen or simply doing something deliberately.
Combatively: That which is done with a lot of struggling. Those who combatively make decisions are the ones who struggle with it.
Complacent state: Where one shows calm satisfaction with himself, his work or his situation.
Creature comforts: All the things needed for a person's comfort, example good food, a nice home or good things in general.

Dd

Devastating: That which causes severe shock, grief or distress.
Dilapidated: That which is in a bad state of repair.
Double-dealers: Those who say one thing and mean another. Dishonest people who deceive others.

Ee

Eminently: Another word for obviously.

Ff
Faltering: Acting in a way that shows lack of confidence. "Faltering between opinions" is to fail to take a decision especially between two things.

Fateful decision: The one whose effect on one's future is very bad.
Fathom: To understand somebody. "It isn't easy to fathom God's ways and thoughts", simply means it is hard to understand them.
Formulate: To create something carefully. To formulate one's thoughts or ideas is to create them carefully with attention to detail.

Gg
Grave in justice: A very serious unfair act on oneself.

Ii
Ill-gotten wealth: Wealth obtained by dishonesty.
Inferiority complex: A feeling that one is less important, less clever or less admired than other people.

Infuse: To fill somebody with a quality.
Intrinsic worth: One's personal qualities such as honor and courage, rather than wealth or social status.
Intuitively: That which happens in a way that does not need conscious reasoning or study.

Jj
Jeopardy: At risk. A person whose life is in jeopardy after making a careless decision is the one who is at risk.

Ll
Long-drawn-out: That which lasts for a very long time.

Mm
Mammon: Wealth regarded as a god or an evil influence.
Meet a long-felt want of many: To give them answers to what they have desired to know. "This book will meet a long-felt want of many" simply means it will answer many people's questions about decision-making.
Momentary: That which happens for a short time.

Pp
Prejudice: Dislike of something that is especially based on false information.
Procrastination: Delaying or postponing action.
Profane: Having or showing contempt for God.

Rr
Resentment: The instance of feeling bitter for example about what one went through in the past.
Ruin: To damage or spoil. "The decisions we make could ruin us permanently or temporarily", simply means they could affect us forever or for a short time.

Ss
Stamina: The ability to endure much physical or mental strain.
Succumb: To fail to resist something.

Tt
Turmoil: State of confusion, great disturbance or uncertainty.

Vv
Virtue of necessity: To make a virtue of necessity is to do something good willingly, even though one has to do it anyway.
Vividly: That which is clear, "it vividly came to past", simply means it happened clearly.
Voyages: Journeys that lead to hell its candidates.

Printed in Great Britain
by Amazon